SDLC Simplified: A Visual and Practical Approach

Mohammad Naushad

Published by Mohammad Naushad, 2025

Copyright

SDLC SIMPLIFIED: A VISUAL AND PRACTICAL APPROACH

First edition. May 1, 2025.

Written by Mohammad Naushad.

Acknowledgements

To every curious mind who has ever wondered, "How is software really built?"—this book is for you.

To the **students** taking their first steps into software development.

To the developers refining their craft, and the **project managers** striving for smoother workflows—may this guide make your journey clearer.

To my mentors, who taught me that complexity can always be simplified.

To my readers, whose hunger for knowledge inspires me to teach.

And to my family, for their endless patience as I turned ideas into these pages.

—Mohammad Naushd

Table of contents

Chapter 1: Book Introduction

Have you ever wondered what goes on behind the scenes when your favorite app gets a new feature, or how that game-changing software solution at work came to be? The world of software development is a fascinating realm where creativity meets technical precision, and ideas transform into digital realities that shape our daily lives. Welcome to "The Complete SDLC Handbook: From Requirements to Maintenance," your comprehensive guide to understanding the intricate dance of software creation from start to finish.

As someone who has spent over two decades in the software industry, I've witnessed firsthand the evolution of development practices and the increasing complexity of digital solutions. I've seen projects soar to great heights and others crash and burn, all hinging on the strength of their development process. That's why I'm thrilled to take you on this journey through the Software Development Life Cycle (SDLC), a framework that has become the backbone of successful software projects worldwide.

But why should you care about SDLC?

In today's digital age, software touches every aspect of our lives. From the alarm app that wakes you up in the morning to the navigation system that guides you home, from the social media platforms that connect you with friends to the financial systems that manage your money – software is omnipresent. Understanding how these tools come to life isn't just interesting; it's essential. Whether you're a budding developer, a project manager, or simply someone curious about the tech world, grasping the SDLC will give you invaluable insights into the digital landscape that surrounds us.

This book is not just another dry, technical manual. It's a practical, engaging exploration of the SDLC that combines real-world examples with cutting-edge methodologies. I've distilled years of experience, countless projects, and the latest industry trends into a guidebook that will transform the way you think about software development. From the spark of an idea to the maintenance of a living, breathing system, we'll cover every phase of the SDLC with depth and clarity.

What sets this book apart is its holistic approach. While many resources focus on specific aspects of software development, "The Complete SDLC Handbook" offers a panoramic view of the entire process. We'll delve into each phase with the detail it deserves, but always with an eye on how it fits into the bigger picture. This comprehensive perspective is crucial in today's interconnected development environments, where decisions made in one phase can have far-reaching impacts on others.

As we embark on this exploration, several key themes will emerge, serving as guiding lights throughout our journey. First and foremost is the concept of iteration. Gone are the days of rigid, linear development processes. Modern SDLC embraces flexibility, allowing for constant refinement and improvement. You'll learn how to build feedback loops into every stage, ensuring that your software evolves alongside user needs and technological advancements.

Another central theme is integration. In the past, different phases of development often operated in silos, leading to miscommunication and inefficiencies. We'll explore how modern SDLC practices break down these barriers, fostering collaboration between teams and ensuring a seamless flow from requirements gathering to deployment and beyond. You'll discover tools and techniques that facilitate this integration, from shared repositories to continuous integration pipelines.

Quality is a thread that runs through every chapter of this book. We'll discuss how to bake quality assurance into each phase of development, rather than treating it as an afterthought. From writing testable requirements to implementing robust testing strategies, you'll learn how to create software that not only meets specifications but exceeds expectations in terms of reliability and user satisfaction.

User-centricity is another key concept we'll explore in depth. In today's competitive software landscape, understanding and meeting user needs is paramount. We'll dive into techniques for gathering and analyzing user requirements, designing intuitive interfaces, and continuously gathering feedback to refine your product. You'll learn how to put the user at the heart of your development process, creating software that truly resonates with its intended audience.

Lastly, we'll focus on adaptability. The tech world moves at breakneck speed, and successful software development requires the ability to pivot quickly in response to new technologies, market changes, or shifting user preferences. Throughout the book, you'll gain insights into creating flexible architectures, implementing agile methodologies, and fostering a culture of innovation that allows your software to evolve and thrive in an ever-changing digital ecosystem.

Who is this book for?

If you're a developer looking to broaden your understanding beyond coding, this book will give you the big-picture perspective needed to advance your career. Project managers will find invaluable insights into coordinating complex development processes and aligning technical work with business goals. Business analysts will discover techniques for bridging the gap between stakeholder needs and technical implementation. Even if you're a non-technical professional working in a tech-adjacent field, this book will demystify the software development process, enabling you to communicate more effectively with technical teams and make informed decisions about software projects.

By the time you finish "The Complete SDLC Handbook," you'll have gained a wealth of knowledge and practical skills. You'll understand how to gather and analyze requirements effectively, ensuring that your projects start on the right foot. You'll be equipped with strategies for designing robust, scalable solutions that can stand the test of time. You'll have a toolkit of development best practices and testing methodologies to ensure your software is of the highest quality. You'll be versed in modern deployment strategies that minimize risk and maximize efficiency. And you'll have insights into maintaining and evolving software systems to keep them relevant and valuable long after their initial release.

But beyond these practical skills, you'll gain something even more valuable: a new way of thinking about software development. You'll see how each decision, from the earliest stages of planning to the ongoing maintenance of a live system, fits into a larger context. This holistic understanding will empower you to make more informed decisions, communicate more effectively across teams, and ultimately contribute to the creation of better software.

As we dive into the world of SDLC, I want you to imagine yourself as part of a grand orchestra. Each musician (or in our case, each phase of development) has its own crucial role to play. But it's only when all these elements come together in harmony that we create something truly beautiful and impactful. That's the power of a well-implemented SDLC – it turns the complex process of software development into a symphonic masterpiece.

Let me share a personal anecdote that illustrates the importance of a comprehensive approach to software development. Early in my career, I was part of a team developing a customer relationship management (CRM) system for a large retail chain. We had brilliant developers, a clear vision from management, and what we thought were well-defined requirements. We worked tirelessly, coding features and fixing bugs, confident that we were creating a game-changing solution.

However, when we finally deployed the system, we were met with a lukewarm reception from the end-users – the sales staff who would be using the CRM daily. Despite its technical sophistication, the system was cumbersome to use and didn't align well with their workflow. We had failed to adequately involve the end-users in the requirements gathering and design phases, and we hadn't conducted thorough user acceptance testing before deployment.

This experience was a wake-up call. It taught me that technical excellence alone isn't enough. Successful software development requires a holistic approach that considers every phase of the SDLC, from initial concept to final deployment and beyond. It needs to balance technical requirements with user needs, project timelines with quality assurance, and current functionality with future scalability.

This book is born out of lessons like these – hard-won insights from real-world experiences. As we explore each phase of the SDLC, I'll share more stories from the trenches, both successes and failures, to illustrate key concepts and provide context for the methodologies we'll discuss.

We'll start our journey with an in-depth look at **requirements gathering**. You'll learn proven techniques for identifying stakeholders, eliciting needs, and documenting requirements in a way that sets your project up for success. We'll explore the art of asking the right questions and the science of analyzing the answers to create a solid foundation for your software project.

From there, we'll delve into the world of **solution design**. You'll discover how to translate requirements into robust architectures that can stand the test of time. We'll explore different design patterns and architectural styles, discussing when and how to apply them to create scalable, maintainable software systems. You'll learn how to balance competing priorities like performance, security, and ease of maintenance to create designs that truly meet the needs of your users and your organization.

As we move into the **development phase**, you'll gain insights into best practices that go beyond just writing code. We'll explore version control strategies, code review processes, and collaboration tools that can dramatically improve the efficiency and quality of your development efforts. You'll learn how to create code that's not just functional, but also readable, maintainable, and adaptable to future needs.

Testing is a critical part of any software project, and we'll give it the attention it deserves. From unit testing to integration testing, from system testing to user acceptance testing, you'll learn strategies for ensuring the quality and reliability of your software at every level. We'll explore both manual and automated testing techniques, and you'll gain insights into creating comprehensive test plans that catch bugs before they reach your users.

Deployment can make or break a software project, and we'll cover it in depth. You'll learn about different deployment strategies, from traditional approaches to modern techniques like blue-green deployments and canary releases. We'll explore the world of continuous integration and continuous deployment (CI/CD), showing you how to create automated pipelines that can take your code from development to production with confidence and speed.

But our journey doesn't end with deployment. In today's fast-paced digital world, launching a software product is just the beginning. We'll dive deep into the often overlooked but crucial phase of **software maintenance and support**. You'll learn strategies for monitoring performance, handling updates and patches, and evolving your software to meet changing needs. We'll also explore approaches to modernizing legacy systems, helping you breathe new life into older software assets.

Throughout the book, we'll keep an eye on the future, discussing **emerging trends** that are shaping the world of software development. From the integration of AI and machine learning into development processes to the rise of low-code and no-code platforms, you'll gain insights into where the industry is heading and how to position yourself and your projects for success in the years to come.

Remember, great software isn't built in a vacuum. It's the result of careful planning, collaborative effort, and a deep understanding of both technical possibilities and human needs. As we journey through each phase of the SDLC, try to imagine how you might apply these concepts to your own projects or organization. Consider the challenges you've faced in the past and how the strategies we discuss might help overcome them.

I encourage you to engage actively with the material. Take notes, reflect on your own experiences, and consider how you might implement these ideas in your work. The true value of this book lies not just in the knowledge it imparts, but in how you apply that knowledge to create better software and more efficient development processes.

As we dive into the first chapter and begin our exploration of the Software Development Life Cycle, I want you to feel a sense of excitement. We're about to embark on a journey that will transform the way you think about software development. You're not just going to learn about a process; you're going to gain insights that will empower you to create digital solutions that can change the world.

So, are you ready to unlock the secrets of successful software development? Are you prepared to gain the knowledge and skills that will set you apart in the fast-paced world of technology? Then let's turn the page and begin our adventure into the heart of the Software Development Life Cycle. The digital world is waiting for your contributions, and with the insights you'll gain from this book, you'll be well-equipped to make your mark. Let's get started!

Chapter 2: Introduction to Software Development Life Cycle (SDLC)

What is SDLC and Why Should You Care?

Picture this: you're tasked with building a house. Would you start by laying the roof? Of course not! You'd begin with a solid foundation, then frame the walls, and so on. The same principle applies to software development. This is where the Software Development Life Cycle, or SDLC, comes into play.

SDLC is like a roadmap for creating software applications. It's a structured approach that guides you through the entire process of developing software, from the initial spark of an idea to the final product and beyond. But why should you care about SDLC? Well, if you're involved in software development in any capacity - whether you're a developer, project manager, or stakeholder - understanding SDLC can be the difference between a successful project and a costly disaster.

The Importance of SDLC: More Than Just a Buzzword

You might be thinking, "Isn't SDLC just another buzzword in the tech industry?" I assure you, it's much more than that. SDLC is the backbone of successful software development. Here's why it's crucial:

Structure and Organization: SDLC provides a clear, step-by-step approach to software development. It's like having a GPS for your project, guiding you from start to finish.

Quality Assurance: By following SDLC, you're building quality into your software from the ground up. It's not just about fixing bugs at the end; it's about preventing them from the beginning.

Risk Management: SDLC helps identify and mitigate risks early in the process. It's like having a safety net for your project.

Cost Efficiency: By planning and organizing your project effectively, SDLC can help reduce costs and prevent budget overruns.

Improved Communication: SDLC provides a common language and framework for all stakeholders, improving communication and reducing misunderstandings.

Overview of SDLC Phases: The Journey from Concept to Reality

Now that you understand the importance of SDLC, let's take a bird's eye view of its phases. Think of these phases as the chapters in your software development story. Each phase builds upon the previous one, creating a cohesive narrative for your project.

SDLC Phases: The Journey from Concept to Reality

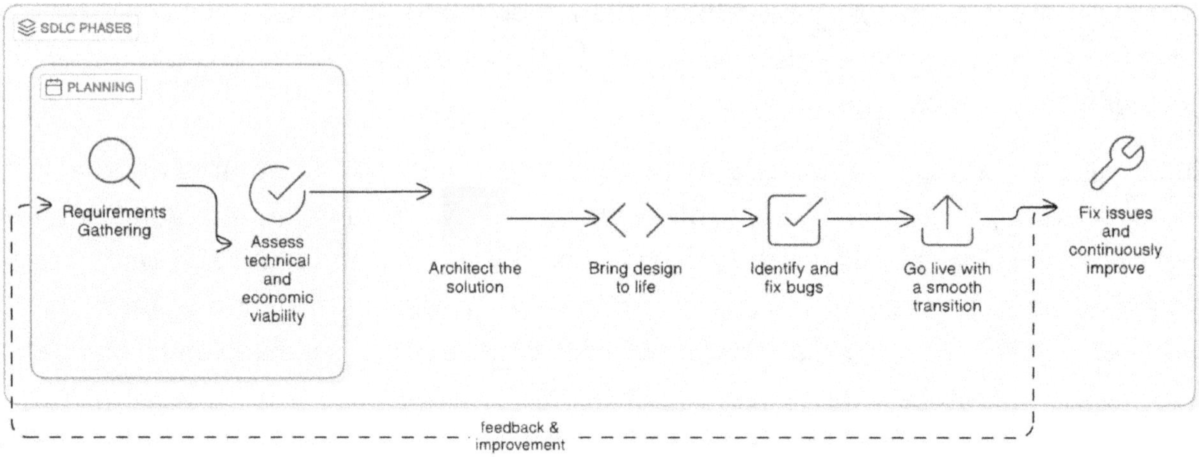

Requirements Gathering: This is where it all begins. You're essentially playing detective, uncovering what the software needs to do and why. It's about asking the right questions and listening carefully to stakeholders.

Feasibility Study: Here, you put on your analyst hat. Is this project technically feasible? Economically viable? Operationally sound? This phase helps you avoid embarking on a journey that's doomed from the start.

Design: This is where your creativity shines. You're architecting the solution, deciding how the software will look and function. It's like creating a blueprint for a house before construction begins.

Development: Now we're getting into the nitty-gritty. This is where the actual coding happens. You're bringing your design to life, one line of code at a time.

Testing: Quality is key, and that's what this phase is all about. You're putting your software through its paces, identifying and fixing bugs, and ensuring it meets all requirements.

Deployment: It's showtime! This is where your software goes live. But it's not just about flipping a switch; it's about ensuring a smooth transition from development to production.

Maintenance: The journey doesn't end with deployment. This phase is about keeping your software running smoothly, fixing issues, and making improvements over time.

Each of these phases has its own set of challenges and best practices, which we'll explore in depth throughout this book. Remember, while these phases are typically sequential, modern SDLC methodologies often involve iterations and overlaps between phases.

Evolution of SDLC Methodologies: From Waterfalls to Agile Sprints

The world of software development is constantly evolving, and so are SDLC methodologies. Let's take a walk through the evolution of SDLC, shall we?

The Waterfall Model: The Classic Approach

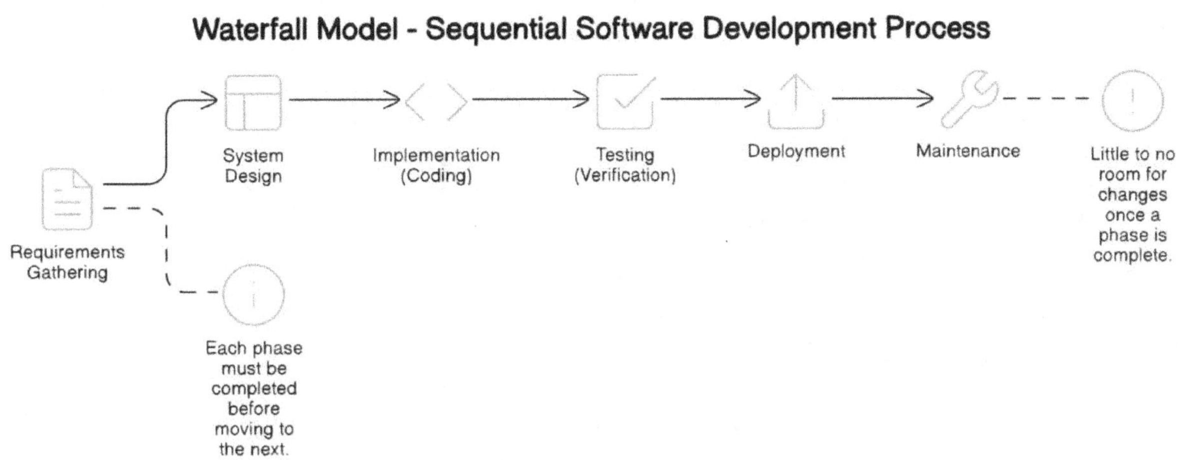

The Waterfall model is where it all began. Introduced in the 1970s, this model follows a linear, sequential approach. Each phase must be completed before moving on to the next, like water flowing down a series of steps.

The Waterfall model was commonly used in earlier software development practices, particularly for projects with well-defined, stable requirements. However, in the fast-paced world of software development, where change is constant, this model often posed challenges when requirements shifted mid-project, making adaptation difficult.

The V-Model: Waterfall with a Twist

The V-Model, introduced in the 1980s, is like the Waterfall model's more sophisticated cousin. It emphasizes the relationship between each development stage and its associated testing phase. This model improved quality assurance but still struggled with flexibility.

V-Model: Verification & Validation in SDLC

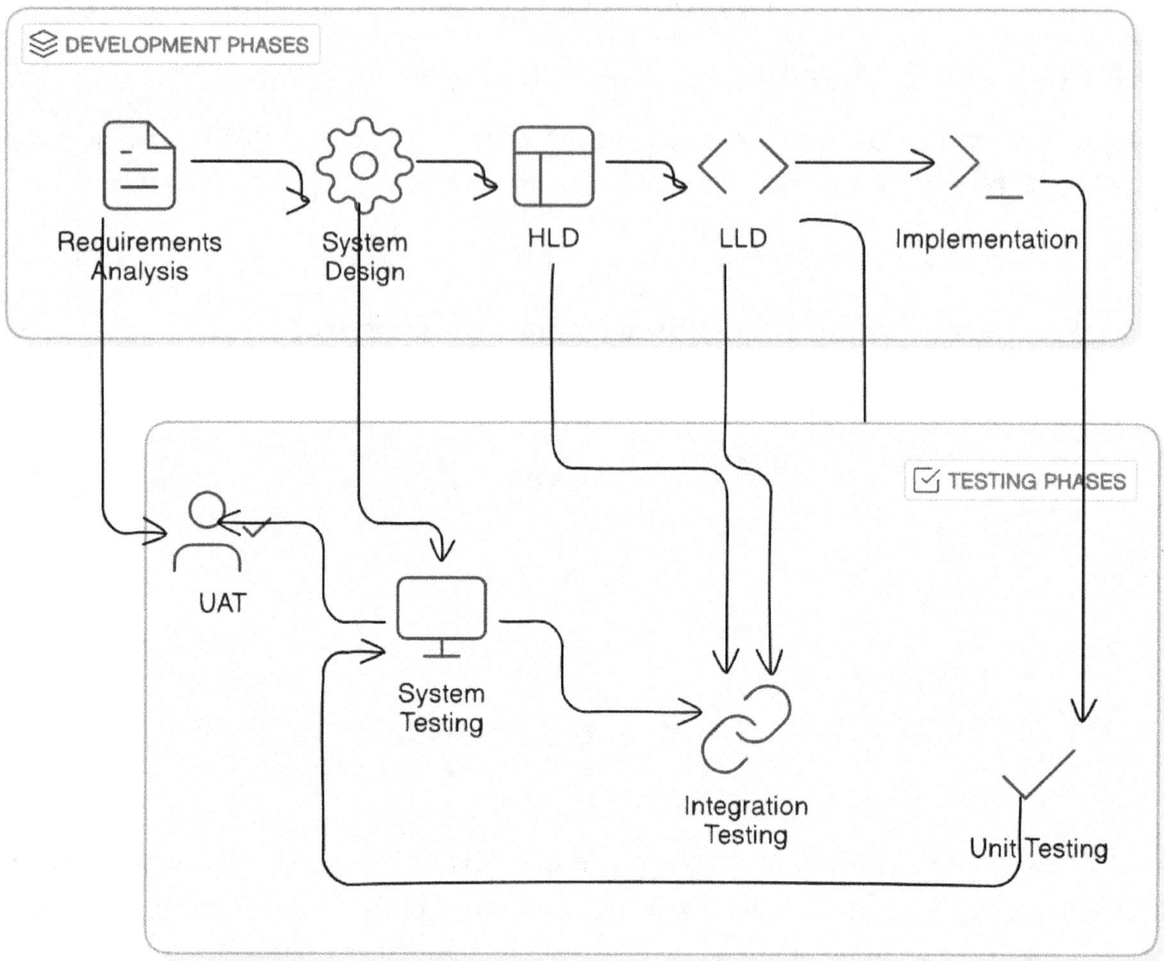

The Spiral Model: Embracing Risk

The Spiral model, developed in the mid-1980s, introduced a risk-driven approach to SDLC. It combines elements of both design and prototyping in stages, allowing for incremental releases of the product and refinement through multiple iterations.

The Spiral model is particularly effective for high-risk projects with significant uncertainties. Its iterative approach, emphasizing risk analysis at each stage, helps teams navigate complexities and deliver successful outcomes.

Spiral Model: Risk-Driven Iterative Development

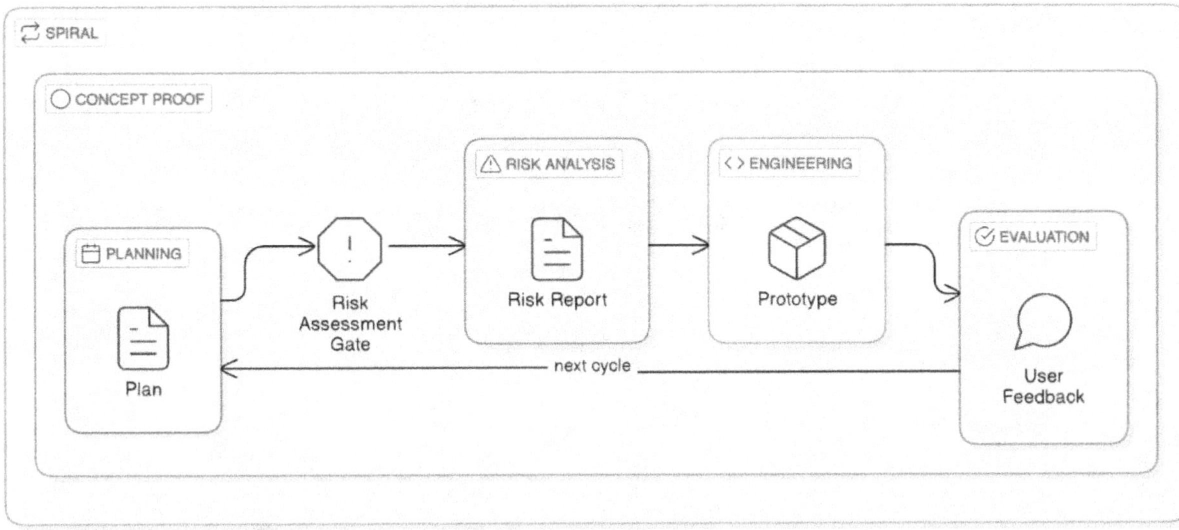

Rapid Application Development (RAD): Speed is Key

Rapid Application Development (RAD) Model - SDLC

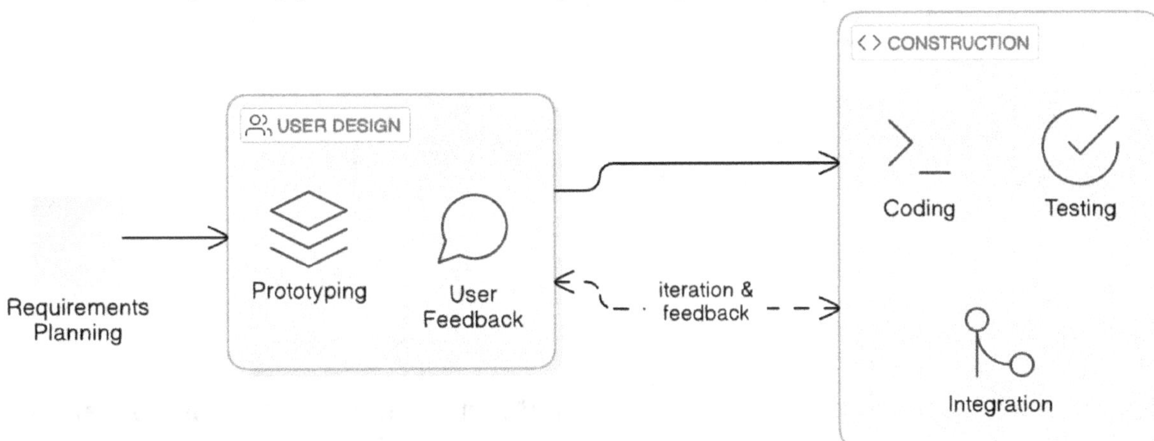

RAD emerged in the 1990s as a response to the need for faster development cycles. It emphasizes rapid prototyping and quick feedback, making it ideal for projects with tight timelines.

Agile: The Game Changer

The Agile methodology, introduced in the early 2000s, revolutionized SDLC. It emphasizes flexibility, customer collaboration, and rapid delivery of working software. Agile breaks the project into small, manageable units called sprints, allowing for frequent reassessment and adaptation. The ability to adapt quickly to changing requirements and deliver value incrementally was a game-changer. However, it also required a significant shift in mindset and team dynamics.

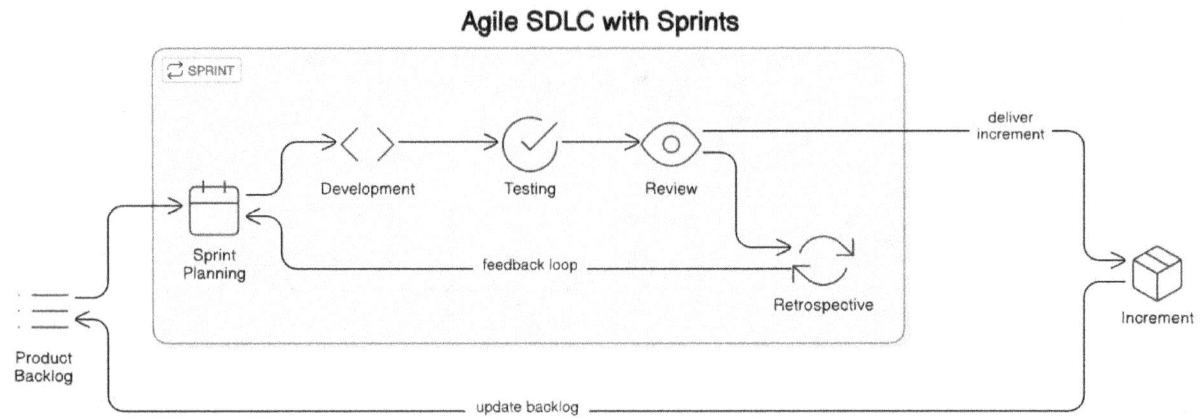

DevOps: Breaking Down Silos

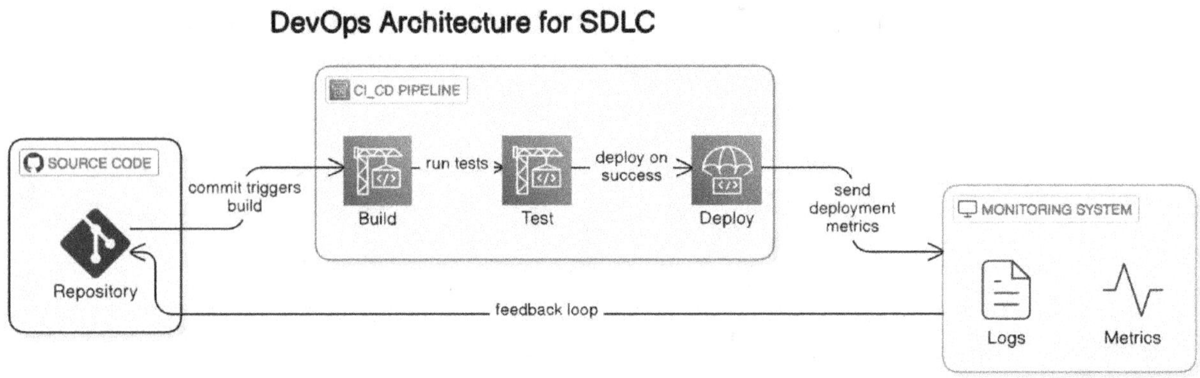

DevOps, a more recent evolution, aims to break down the barriers between development and operations teams. It emphasizes collaboration, automation, and continuous delivery.

Adopting DevOps practices enables faster deployments, improved quality, and stronger team collaboration. However, it demands a cultural shift and investment in automation tools to achieve these benefits.

Choosing the Right SDLC Methodology: One Size Doesn't Fit All

With all these methodologies, you might be wondering, "Which one should I choose?" The truth is, there's no one-size-fits-all answer. The best methodology depends on various factors:

Project Complexity: Is it a simple application or a complex system with many moving parts?

Timeline: Do you have a fixed deadline, or is there flexibility?

Budget: How much resources can you allocate to the project?

Team Size and Expertise: What's the size of your team, and what are their skill levels?

Client Involvement: How much involvement do stakeholders want in the development process?

Risk Tolerance: How much uncertainty can your project handle?

Projects often fail when the wrong methodology is selected—such as applying a rigid Waterfall approach to projects with evolving requirements or adopting Agile without team alignment. The key is assessing a project's unique needs and selecting the most suitable methodology.

The Future of SDLC: Embracing Change and Innovation

As we look to the future, SDLC continues to evolve. Here are some trends I believe will shape the future of software development:

AI and Machine Learning Integration: AI will play a bigger role in various SDLC phases, from requirements analysis to testing and maintenance.

Low-Code and No-Code Platforms: These platforms are democratizing software development, allowing non-programmers to create applications.

Increased Automation: More aspects of the SDLC will be automated, from code generation to testing and deployment.

Enhanced Security Focus: With increasing cyber threats, security will be integrated more tightly into every phase of SDLC.

Sustainability Considerations: Environmental impact will become a key factor in software design and development decisions.

Conclusion: Your SDLC Journey Begins Here

As we wrap up this introduction to SDLC, I hope you're feeling excited about the journey ahead. Whether you're a seasoned developer or just starting in the world of software development, understanding SDLC is crucial for success.

Remember, SDLC is not just a set of rules to follow blindly. It's a framework that you can adapt and mold to fit your specific needs. As you progress through this book, you'll gain a deeper understanding of each SDLC phase and the best practices associated with them.

In the next chapter, we'll dive deep into the art of requirements gathering. We'll explore techniques to identify stakeholders, elicit requirements effectively, and document them in a way that sets your project up for success. So, buckle up and get ready to master the craft of software development!

Chapter 3: Requirements Gathering Techniques

Introduction

Welcome to the exciting world of requirements gathering! If you're reading this, you're about to embark on a journey that will make or break your software development project. I've been in your shoes, and let me tell you, mastering the art of requirements gathering is like finding the Holy Grail of software development. It's that important.

In this chapter, we're going to dive deep into the techniques that will help you uncover, document, and prioritize the requirements that will shape your software project. Think of it as detective work – you're piecing together clues from various sources to build a complete picture of what your software needs to do. And trust me, it's a lot more fun than it sounds!

Stakeholder Identification and Analysis

Who Are Your Stakeholders?

Let's start with a fundamental question: who are your stakeholders? In simple terms, stakeholders are anyone who has a vested interest in your project. They're the people who will use the software, pay for it, maintain it, or be affected by it in some way.

A common mistake in projects is overlooking key stakeholders during planning. For example, while store managers, IT, and finance teams may be considered critical end-users like warehouse staff might be neglected—leading to major issues. The key lesson? Conduct thorough stakeholder identification to ensure all impacted parties are included.

Here's a quick checklist to help you identify stakeholders:

1. End-users
2. Project sponsors
3. Management

4. IT department
5. Customer service representatives
6. External partners or vendors
7. Regulatory bodies (if applicable)

Stakeholder Analysis: Not All Stakeholders Are Created Equal

Once you've identified your stakeholders, it's time to analyze them. Not all stakeholders will have the same level of influence or interest in your project. Your job is to figure out who's who.

A simple but effective tool for this is the Power/Interest Grid. Here's how it works:

1. Draw a 2x2 grid
2. Label the horizontal axis "Interest" (low to high)
3. Label the vertical axis "Power" (low to high)
4. Place each stakeholder in the appropriate quadrant

This visual representation will help you prioritize your engagement with different stakeholders. For instance, stakeholders with high power and high interest (let's call them your VIPs) will need more frequent and detailed communication than those with low power and low interest.

Elicitation Methods: The Art of Extracting Information

Now that you know who your stakeholders are, it's time to start gathering those precious requirements. There are several methods at your disposal, and I'll walk you through the most effective ones.

Interviews: One-on-One Deep Dives

Interviews are like first dates with your stakeholders – a chance to get to know them and their needs on a deeper level. I've found that one-on-one interviews are particularly effective for gathering detailed information and uncovering hidden requirements.

Tips for effective interviews:

1. Prepare a list of open-ended questions
2. Listen more than you talk
3. Use the "5 Whys" technique to dig deeper

4. Take notes or record the conversation (with permission)
5. Follow up with a summary to ensure you understood correctly

Remember, the goal is to understand not just what the stakeholder wants, but why they want it. I once interviewed a client who insisted on a particular feature, and it was only after asking "why" several times that we uncovered the real requirement – which was actually solved by a much simpler solution.

Surveys: Casting a Wide Net

Surveys are great when you need to gather information from a large number of stakeholders quickly. They're particularly useful for quantitative data and for identifying trends or patterns in requirements.

Here are some best practices for creating effective surveys:

1. Keep it short and focused
2. Use a mix of question types (multiple choice, rating scales, open-ended)
3. Pilot test your survey with a small group
4. Provide clear instructions and definitions
5. Offer an incentive for completion if possible

Surveys can reveal surprising insights during user interface redesigns—features assumed to be crucial may turn out to be rarely used, while seemingly minor elements often prove essential to users. This highlights the importance of user feedback in prioritizing design decisions.

Workshops: Collaborative Requirement Gathering

Workshops are like the potluck dinners of requirement gathering – everyone brings something to the table. They're fantastic for fostering collaboration, generating ideas, and resolving conflicts between different stakeholders.

Here's how to run an effective requirements workshop:

1. Set clear objectives for the session
2. Invite the right mix of stakeholders
3. Use visual aids (whiteboards, sticky notes, etc.)
4. Employ techniques like brainstorming or affinity mapping

5. Have a skilled facilitator to keep things on track

Requirements workshops consistently demonstrate their value by fostering collaboration among stakeholders. The dynamic exchange of perspectives often sparks innovative solutions and uncovers critical requirements that might otherwise remain overlooked. This collaborative approach proves particularly effective for identifying comprehensive project needs.

Observation: Walking in Your Users' Shoes

Sometimes, the best way to understand requirements is to see them in action. Observation involves watching users in their natural environment as they perform their tasks.

Tips for effective observation:

1. Be as unobtrusive as possible
2. Take detailed notes or use a predefined observation form
3. Pay attention to workarounds or pain points
4. Follow up with questions to clarify what you've observed

Direct observation in real-world settings can uncover critical, unspoken requirements that traditional interviews or surveys might miss. Shadowing end-users—such as nurses in a hospital—often reveals essential workflow nuances and unmet needs that significantly improve system design.

Documenting Requirements: Turning Chaos into Order

Congratulations! You've gathered a wealth of information from your stakeholders. Now comes the challenging part – turning all that raw data into clear, actionable requirements.

User Stories: Putting the User First

User stories are a popular way of documenting requirements, especially in Agile environments. They follow a simple format:

As a [type of user], I want [an action] so that [a benefit/a value].

For example: "As a online shopper, I want to save items to a wishlist so that I can easily find and purchase them later."

User stories are great because they keep the focus on the user and the value they're trying to achieve. They're also easy for non-technical stakeholders to understand and validate.

Use Cases: Mapping Out the Details

Use cases provide a more detailed view of how a user interacts with the system to achieve a specific goal. They typically include:

1. Actor (who is performing the action)
2. Preconditions
3. Main flow of events
4. Alternative flows
5. Postconditions

Use cases are particularly useful for complex interactions or when you need to capture detailed business rules.

Functional vs. Non-Functional Requirements

It's important to document both functional and non-functional requirements:

- Functional requirements describe what the system should do
- Non-functional requirements describe how the system should perform

For example, "The system shall allow users to reset their password" is a functional requirement, while "The system shall load pages in less than 2 seconds" is a non-functional requirement.

Requirements Traceability Matrix

A Requirements Traceability Matrix (RTM) is a document that maps requirements to their sources and to the project deliverables that satisfy them. It's a powerful tool for ensuring that all requirements are accounted for and for managing changes throughout the project lifecycle.

Prioritizing Requirements: The Art of Saying No

In an ideal world, we'd be able to implement every requirement our stakeholders ask for. In reality, we have to make tough choices. Prioritization is about deciding which requirements are must-haves and which are nice-to-haves.

MoSCoW Method

The MoSCoW method is a simple but effective prioritization technique. It stands for:

- Must have

- Should have
- Could have
- Won't have (this time)

This method helps you focus on the essential requirements while keeping track of less critical ones for future iterations.

Kano Model

The Kano Model is another useful prioritization tool. It categorizes requirements into:

1. Basic features (must-haves)
2. Performance features (the more, the better)
3. Excitement features (unexpected delighters)

This model helps you balance between meeting basic expectations and delivering features that will wow your users.

Cost-Benefit Analysis

Sometimes, the best way to prioritize is to look at the numbers. A cost-benefit analysis involves estimating the cost of implementing each requirement and the potential benefit it will bring. This can help you identify the "low-hanging fruit" – requirements that offer high value for relatively low cost.

Common Pitfalls in Requirements Gathering

Before we wrap up, let's talk about some common pitfalls to avoid:

1. Assuming you know what the users want without asking them
2. Focusing solely on functional requirements and neglecting non-functional ones
3. Failing to involve all relevant stakeholders
4. Not validating requirements with stakeholders
5. Trying to gather all requirements upfront instead of iterating

Avoid common pitfalls in requirements gathering—learning from these mistakes early can save significant time and effort. Being aware of these challenges helps ensure a smoother and more effective process.

Conclusion: Requirements gathering is both an art and a science. It requires technical skills, people skills, and a good dose of detective work. But with the techniques we've covered in this chapter, you're well-equipped to tackle this crucial phase of the software development lifecycle.
Remember, good requirements are the foundation of successful software projects. Take the time to get them right, and you'll save yourself countless headaches down the road.

As we move into the next chapter on conducting feasibility studies, keep in mind that the requirements you've gathered will play a crucial role in determining the feasibility of your project. So pat yourself on the back for a job well done, and let's dive into the world of feasibility analysis!

Chapter 4: Conducting Feasibility Studies

Introduction

Welcome to Chapter 3, where we'll dive deep into the world of feasibility studies. If you've ever wondered how to determine whether your software project is viable before investing significant time and resources, you're in the right place. I've been in your shoes, facing the daunting task of assessing project feasibility, and I'm here to guide you through this crucial phase of the Software Development Life Cycle (SDLC).

Feasibility studies are like the compass that keeps your project on course. They help you navigate the treacherous waters of software development by identifying potential obstacles and opportunities before you set sail. In this chapter, we'll explore the different types of feasibility studies, learn how to conduct a cost-benefit analysis, and develop strategies for assessing and mitigating risks.

So, grab your explorer's hat, and let's embark on this journey together!

Types of Feasibility Studies

When it comes to feasibility studies, one size doesn't fit all. There are several types of feasibility studies, each focusing on a different aspect of your project. Let's break them down:

Technical Feasibility

Technical feasibility is all about answering the question: "Can we build it?" It's like assessing whether you have the right tools and materials to construct a house before breaking ground.

In this study, you'll evaluate:

1. The availability of required technology
2. The technical expertise of your team
3. The compatibility with existing systems
4. The scalability of the proposed solution

Implementing cutting-edge AI systems requires careful technical feasibility assessments. Even when technology is available, teams may lack the necessary expertise—highlighting the importance of evaluating skillsets and investing in training before project execution.

To conduct a technical feasibility study:

1. List all the technical requirements of your project
2. Assess your team's current skills and knowledge
3. Identify any gaps between requirements and capabilities
4. Research potential solutions to bridge these gaps
5. Estimate the time and resources needed to acquire necessary technology or skills

Economic Feasibility

Economic feasibility addresses the question: "Should we build it?" This study helps you determine if the project makes financial sense.

Key aspects of economic feasibility include:

1. Development costs
2. Operational costs
3. Return on Investment (ROI)
4. Break-even analysis

Initial project enthusiasm can sometimes overshadow economic realities. A thorough economic feasibility study often reveals critical financial constraints—such as extended breakeven periods—prompting necessary pivots to more viable alternatives.

To conduct an economic feasibility study:

1. Estimate all costs associated with the project (development, implementation, maintenance)

2. Project potential revenues or cost savings
3. Calculate the ROI and payback period
4. Compare the project's financial performance to alternatives

Operational Feasibility

Operational feasibility answers the question: "If we build it, will they come?" This study assesses how well the proposed system will work in your organization and whether it will be used effectively.

Factors to consider in operational feasibility include:

1. User acceptance
2. Organizational culture
3. Existing operational procedures
4. Training requirements

Even technically sound and economically viable projects can fail without proper operational feasibility analysis. Overlooking user adoption challenges—such as system complexity—often leads to implementation difficulties and resistance.

To conduct an operational feasibility study:

1. Identify key stakeholders and end-users
2. Assess current operational procedures
3. Evaluate the impact of the new system on existing processes
4. Gauge user acceptance through surveys or interviews
5. Determine training needs and change management requirements

Cost-Benefit Analysis

Now that we've explored the types of feasibility studies, let's dive into one of the most crucial aspects of economic feasibility: the cost-benefit analysis. This is where we put on our accountant hats and crunch some numbers.

Identifying Costs

The first step in a cost-benefit analysis is to identify all the costs associated with your project. These can be broadly categorized into:

1. Direct costs: These are expenses directly tied to the project, such as:
   - Hardware and software purchases
   - Development team salaries
   - Training expenses
   - Licensing fees
2. Indirect costs: These are less obvious but still important, including:
   - Overhead costs (electricity, office space)
   - Opportunity costs (what you're giving up by pursuing this project)
   - Potential disruptions to existing operations
3. Ongoing costs: Don't forget about expenses that continue after implementation:
   - Maintenance and support
   - Updates and upgrades
   - Operational costs

Cloud hosting solutions may appear cost-effective initially but can lead to substantial long-term expenses if ongoing costs aren't accounted for. A comprehensive cost analysis should always include recurring operational expenses to avoid budget overruns!

Quantifying Benefits

Next, we need to identify and quantify the benefits of the project. This can be trickier than identifying costs, as some benefits are intangible. Here's how you can approach it:

1. Tangible benefits: These are easier to quantify and may include:
   - Increased revenue
   - Cost savings
   - Improved productivity
   - Reduced error rates
2. Intangible benefits: These are harder to put a number on but are still important:
   - Enhanced customer satisfaction
   - Improved brand image

- Better employee morale
- Competitive advantage

To quantify intangible benefits, you might need to get creative. For example, you could estimate the value of improved customer satisfaction by projecting increased customer retention rates.

Calculating ROI

Once you have your costs and benefits identified and quantified, it's time to calculate the Return on Investment (ROI). The basic formula is:

ROI = (Net Benefits / Total Costs) x 100

For example, if your project costs $100,000 and is expected to generate $150,000 in benefits over its lifetime, your ROI would be:

ROI = ($150,000 - $100,000) / $100,000 x 100 = 50%

This means for every dollar invested, you're getting 50 cents in return.

Net Present Value (NPV)

While ROI is useful, it doesn't account for the time value of money. That's where Net Present Value (NPV) comes in. NPV calculates the present value of all future cash flows, both positive and negative.

The formula for NPV is:

NPV = Σ (Benefits - Costs) / (1 + r)^t

Where:

- Σ is the sum
- r is the discount rate
- t is the time period

A positive NPV indicates that the project is financially viable.

Break-Even Analysis

Another useful tool in your cost-benefit arsenal is the break-even analysis. This tells you how long it will take for your project to start generating a positive return.

To calculate the break-even point:

1. Determine your fixed costs
2. Estimate your variable costs per unit
3. Calculate your revenue per unit
4. Use the formula: Break-even point = Fixed Costs / (Revenue per unit - Variable costs per unit)

This will give you the number of units you need to sell (or the amount of time needed) to break even.

Remember, the goal of a cost-benefit analysis is not just to determine if a project is profitable, but to compare it with other potential projects or the option of doing nothing. Always consider opportunity costs in your analysis.

Risk Assessment and Mitigation Strategies

Now that we've crunched the numbers, it's time to put on our detective hats and dive into risk assessment and mitigation. No project is without risks, but identifying and planning for them can mean the difference between success and failure.

Identifying Risks

The first step in risk assessment is identifying potential risks. I like to use the PESTLE framework to ensure we're covering all bases:

1. Political: Changes in government policies or regulations
2. Economic: Market fluctuations, economic downturns
3. Social: Changes in customer behavior or societal trends
4. Technological: Rapid technological changes, obsolescence
5. Legal: Compliance issues, potential lawsuits
6. Environmental: Natural disasters, environmental regulations

In addition to these external factors, don't forget about internal risks such as:

- Resource constraints
- Technical challenges
- Team dynamics

- Scope creep

Failing to identify key personnel risks—like unexpected team departures—can lead to project delays and disruptions. Proactive risk assessment should account for critical resource dependencies to maintain project continuity.

Assessing Risk Impact and Probability

Once you've identified potential risks, it's time to assess their potential impact and probability. A simple way to do this is by using a risk matrix:

1. Assign an impact score (1-5, with 5 being the highest impact)
2. Assign a probability score (1-5, with 5 being the most likely)
3. Multiply these scores to get a risk score

For example, a risk with high impact (5) but low probability (2) would have a risk score of 10.

Prioritizing Risks

Now that you have risk scores, you can prioritize your risks. Generally, you'll want to focus on risks with the highest scores first. However, don't ignore low-probability, high-impact risks entirely. These "black swan" events can be catastrophic if they occur.

Developing Mitigation Strategies

For each prioritized risk, develop a mitigation strategy. There are four main approaches:

1. Avoid: Eliminate the risk by changing your approach
2. Transfer: Shift the risk to another party (e.g., through insurance)
3. Mitigate: Reduce the impact or probability of the risk
4. Accept: Acknowledge the risk and be prepared to deal with consequences if it occurs

Let's look at an example:

Risk: Key team member leaves the project

Impact: 4

Probability: 3

Risk Score: 12

Mitigation strategies:

1. Avoid: Cross-train team members to reduce dependence on any individual
2. Transfer: Engage a staffing agency to quickly provide replacements if needed
3. Mitigate: Document processes and knowledge to ease transition
4. Accept: Build buffer time into the project schedule to account for potential disruptions

Continuous Risk Monitoring

Remember, risk assessment isn't a one-time activity. As your project progresses, new risks may emerge while others become less relevant. Regularly revisit your risk assessment and adjust your strategies as needed.

Making risk review a standing agenda item in project meetings helps maintain team vigilance and enables timely adjustments. This practice ensures continuous risk awareness and proactive mitigation throughout the project lifecycle.

Putting It All Together: The Feasibility Report

Now that we've explored the different types of feasibility studies, conducted a cost-benefit analysis, and assessed risks, it's time to put it all together in a comprehensive feasibility report. This document will be your guide (and potentially your lifesaver) as you move forward with your project.

Structure of a Feasibility Report

A well-structured feasibility report typically includes the following sections:

1. Executive Summary
2. Project Overview
3. Technical Feasibility
4. Economic Feasibility
5. Operational Feasibility
6. Cost-Benefit Analysis
7. Risk Assessment and Mitigation Strategies
8. Conclusions and Recommendations

Let's break these down:

1. Executive Summary

This is a brief overview of your entire report. It should be concise (no more than a page) and highlight the key findings and recommendations. Remember, some stakeholders may only read this section, so make it count!

2. Project Overview

Provide context for the feasibility study. Include:

- Project objectives
- Scope
- Stakeholders
- Timeline

3. Technical Feasibility

Summarize your findings regarding the technical aspects of the project:

- Required technologies
- Team capabilities
- Integration with existing systems
- Scalability considerations

4. Economic Feasibility

Present the financial analysis of the project:

- Development and operational costs
- Projected benefits
- ROI and NPV calculations
- Break-even analysis

5. Operational Feasibility

Discuss how the project fits into the organization's operations:

- Impact on current processes
- User acceptance projections
- Training requirements

- Organizational culture considerations

6. Cost-Benefit Analysis

Provide a detailed breakdown of your cost-benefit analysis:

- Itemized costs (direct, indirect, ongoing)
- Quantified benefits (tangible and intangible)
- Comparison with alternatives (including the option of doing nothing)

7. Risk Assessment and Mitigation Strategies

Present your risk analysis:

- Identified risks (with impact and probability scores)
- Prioritized risk list
- Mitigation strategies for high-priority risks
- Plan for ongoing risk monitoring

8. Conclusions and Recommendations

Based on all the above, provide your overall assessment of the project's feasibility. Be clear about your recommendations - should the project proceed as planned, be modified, or be abandoned?

Tips for Writing an Effective Feasibility Report

1. Be objective: Your job is to present facts and analysis, not to advocate for a particular outcome.
2. Use visuals: Charts, graphs, and tables can make complex information more digestible.
3. Be thorough but concise: Provide enough detail to support your conclusions, but don't overwhelm readers with unnecessary information.
4. Consider your audience: Tailor the level of technical detail to your readers. You might need to create different versions for technical and non-technical stakeholders.
5. Be clear about assumptions: Clearly state any assumptions you've made in your analysis.

6. Provide actionable recommendations: Don't just present problems - suggest solutions.

Conclusion

Conducting a thorough feasibility study is like giving your project a health check-up before it even starts. It helps you identify potential issues, understand the financial implications, and prepare for risks before they become problems.

Remember, the goal of a feasibility study isn't to prove that your project idea is perfect. It's to honestly assess whether the project is viable and worth pursuing. Sometimes, the most valuable outcome of a feasibility study is the decision not to proceed with a project that looked great on the surface but wouldn't stand up to real-world challenges.

As we wrap up this chapter, I hope you feel equipped to conduct your own feasibility studies. In the next chapter, we'll move on to the exciting world of solution design, where we'll take our validated project ideas and start turning them into reality.

But before we do, take a moment to reflect on what we've covered. Think about a project you're currently working on or planning. How might a feasibility study change your approach? What risks haven't you considered? What hidden costs or benefits might you uncover?

Remember, in the world of software development, knowledge is power. The more you know about your project's feasibility, the better positioned you'll be to make it a success. So go forth, analyze, assess, and may all your projects be feasible!

Chapter 5: Principles of Solution Design

Introduction: The Blueprint of Success

Picture this: you're about to embark on a journey to build your dream house. You wouldn't just grab a hammer and start nailing boards together, would you? Of course not! You'd start with a carefully crafted blueprint that outlines every detail of your future home. Well, my friend, solution design in software development is no different. It's the blueprint that sets the foundation for your entire project's success.

In this chapter, we're going to dive deep into the principles of solution design. I'll guide you through the intricate world of architectural patterns, design considerations, and documentation techniques that will help you create robust, scalable, and efficient software solutions. So, grab your virtual hard hat, and let's start building the framework for your next great software project!

Chapter 5: Principles of Solution Design

Architectural Patterns and Styles: Choosing Your Foundation

When it comes to solution design, architectural patterns and styles are like the different types of foundations you can choose for your house. Each has its strengths and is suited for different types of "buildings" or, in our case, software applications.

The Monolithic Architecture: The Classic Bungalow

Let's start with the monolithic architecture. It's like building a classic bungalow – everything under one roof. In this pattern, all components of your application are tightly integrated and run as a single unit.

We chose a monolithic architecture because it was straightforward to develop and deploy. The entire application – from the user interface to the database operations – was bundled together. It worked great... until it didn't.

As the company grew, we found ourselves struggling with scalability issues. Making changes became a nightmare because even a small update required redeploying the entire application. It was like trying to renovate your kitchen but having to tear down and rebuild the whole house!

Pros of Monolithic Architecture:

- Simple to develop for small applications
- Easier to test and deploy initially
- Straightforward to scale horizontally for simple applications

Cons of Monolithic Architecture:

- Becomes complex and hard to understand as the application grows
- Challenging to implement changes and new technologies
- Scaling can be difficult for complex applications

Microservices Architecture: The Modern Apartment Complex

Now, let's talk about microservices architecture. If monolithic is a bungalow, microservices is like a modern apartment complex. Each apartment (or service) is independent but part of the larger structure.

In microservices, your application is broken down into smaller, loosely coupled services that can be developed, deployed, and scaled independently. Each service is responsible for a specific business capability.

Evolution: Monolith to Microservices Architecture

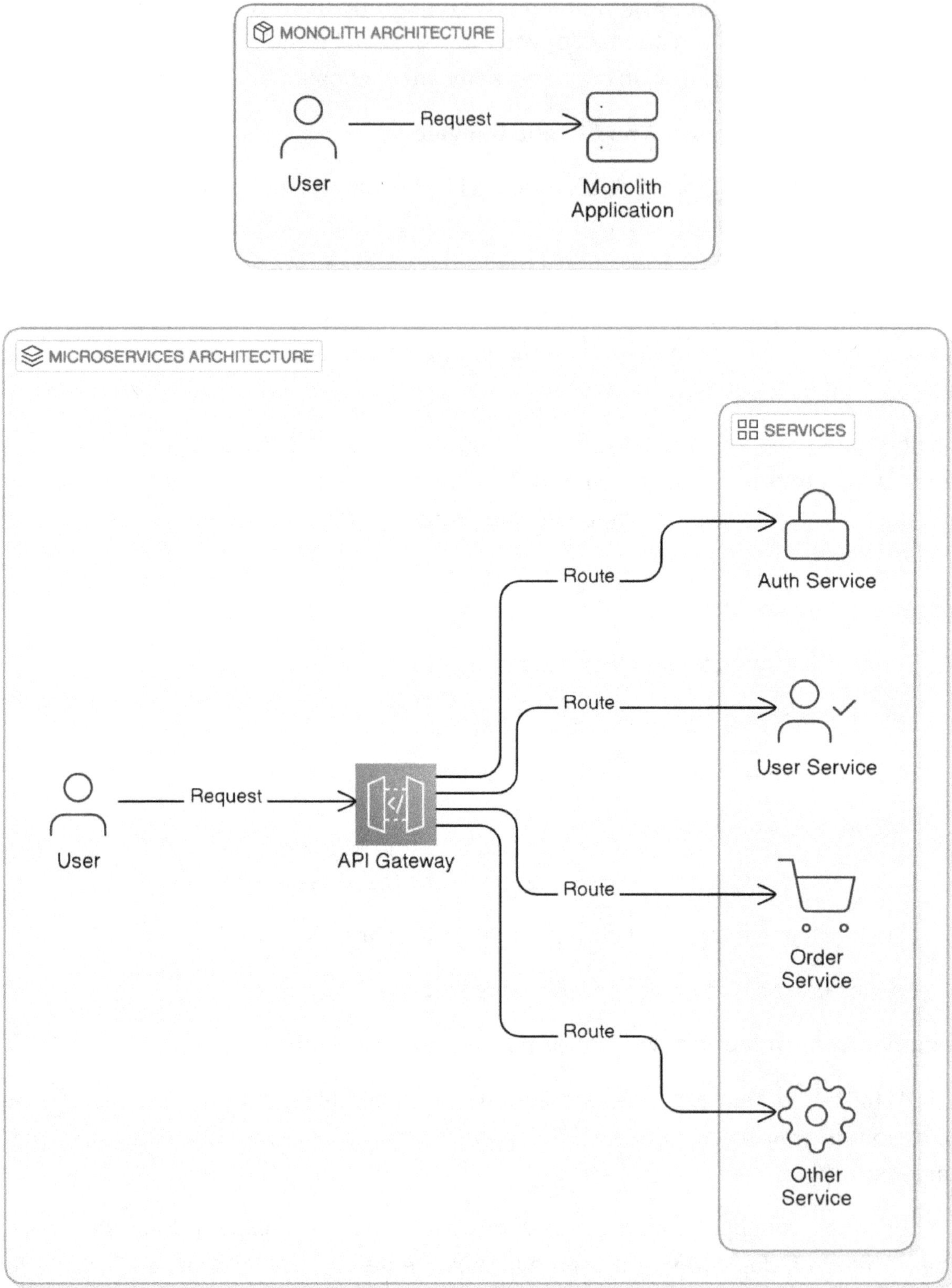

For a large streaming platform where we transitioned from a monolithic to a microservices architecture. It was like breaking our big, clunky bungalow into sleek, efficient apartments. We had separate services for user authentication, content delivery, recommendation engine, and billing.

The result? We could update and scale each service independently. When we needed to handle more users, we scaled up the authentication service. When we added new content, we only touched the content delivery service. It was a game-changer!

Pros of Microservices Architecture:

- Highly scalable and flexible
- Enables use of different technologies for different services
- Easier to understand and maintain individual services
- Supports independent deployment of services

Cons of Microservices Architecture:

- More complex to set up initially
- Requires strong DevOps practices
- Can be overkill for simple applications

Event-Driven Architecture: The Smart Home

Event-driven architecture is like building a smart home. Everything in the house reacts to events – when you enter a room, the lights turn on; when it's too warm, the AC kicks in.

In software terms, an event-driven architecture is built around the production, detection, and reaction to events. Components in the system communicate through events, which allows for loose coupling and high scalability.

Real-time analytics platforms for social media often leverage event-driven architectures, where user actions (posts, likes, comments) generate events. These events are processed by multiple services to instantly update feeds, trigger notifications, and compute analytics, enabling responsive and dynamic user experiences.

Pros of Event-Driven Architecture:

- Highly scalable and responsive
- Excellent for real-time data processing

- Supports easy addition of new features without modifying existing ones

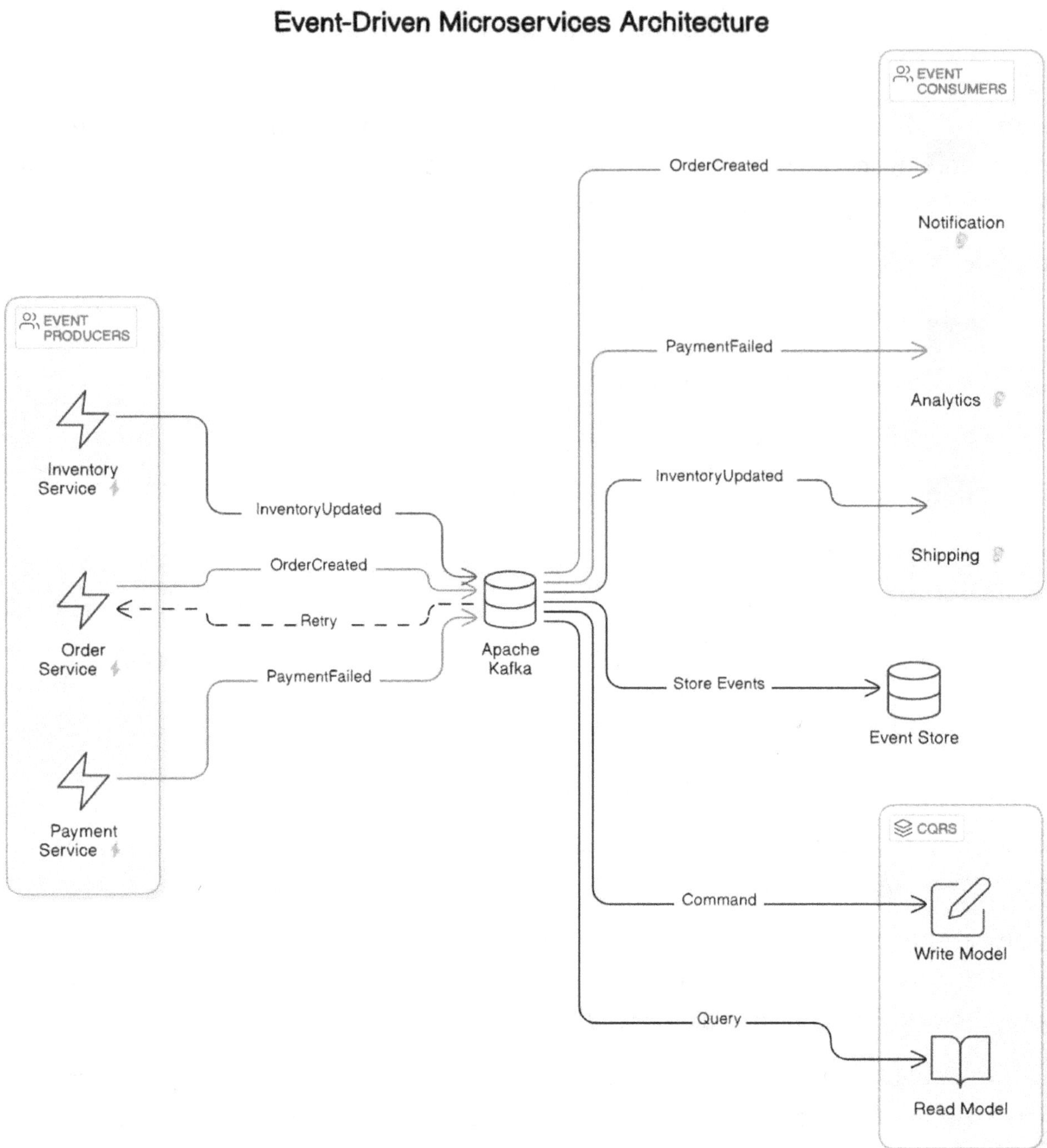

Cons of Event-Driven Architecture:

- Can be complex to design and debug
- Requires careful event management to prevent overwhelming the system
- May lead to eventual consistency, which can be challenging to handle

Layered Architecture: The Multi-Story Office Building

Layered architecture is like constructing a multi-story office building. Each floor has a specific purpose, and they all work together to form the complete structure.

In this pattern, the application is divided into layers, each with a specific role. Typically, you'll see layers like presentation (UI), business logic, and data access. Each layer can only communicate with the layers directly above or below it.

It's great for organizing complex business logic and maintaining a clear separation of concerns. However, changes that span multiple layers can be time-consuming to implement.

Pros of Layered Architecture:

- Clear separation of concerns
- Easy to standardize
- Supports the development of reusable components

Cons of Layered Architecture:

- Can lead to unnecessary complexity for simple applications
- Changes spanning multiple layers can be cumbersome
- Lower layers might become a bottleneck

Remember, there's no one-size-fits-all solution in architecture. The best pattern for your project depends on your specific requirements, team skills, and scalability needs. Don't be afraid to mix and match patterns to create a hybrid architecture that best suits your needs!

Design Considerations: Building for the Future

Now that we've explored different architectural styles, let's talk about the key considerations you need to keep in mind when designing your solution. These are like the building codes and regulations you need to follow to ensure your software "building" is safe, efficient, and future-proof.

Scalability: Room to Grow

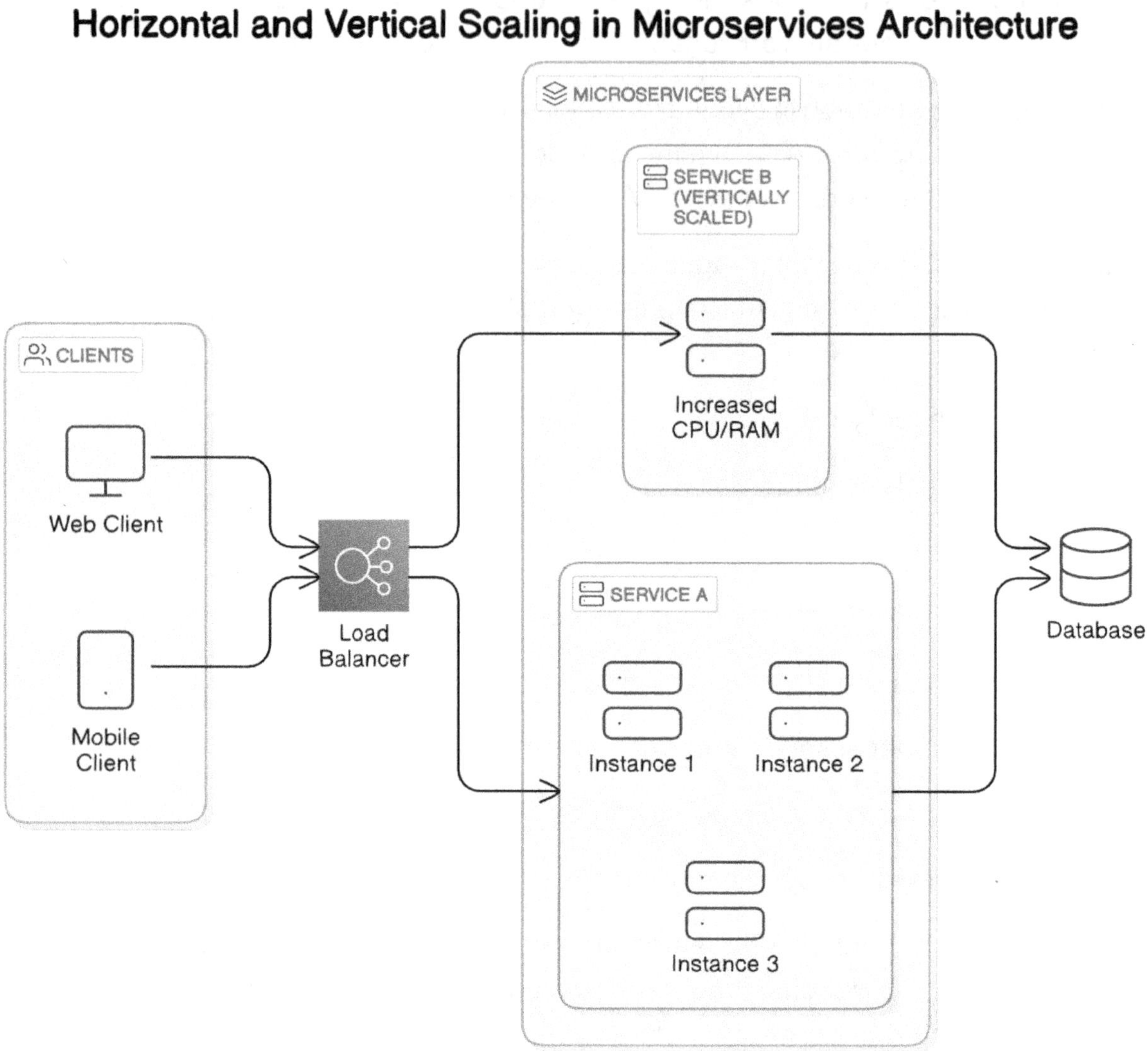

Imagine you're designing a house for a young couple who's planning to have children. You wouldn't just design for their current needs, right? You'd plan for future expansion. The same principle applies to software design.

Scalability is about ensuring your system can handle growth – more users, more data, more features – without a significant drop in performance or a complete overhaul of the architecture.

Scalability is critical when building applications—systems not designed for growth risk crashing under sudden success, leading to poor performance and frustrated users. Proactive scaling strategies prevent costly reactive fixes and maintain user satisfaction.

Here are some key scalability considerations:

1. Horizontal vs. Vertical Scaling: Decide whether you'll scale by adding more machines (horizontal) or by upgrading existing machines (vertical).
2. Stateless Design: Design your components to be stateless where possible. This makes it easier to add or remove instances as needed.
3. Caching: Implement caching strategies to reduce the load on your databases and improve response times.
4. Database Sharding: Consider splitting your data across multiple databases to handle large volumes of data.
5. Asynchronous Processing: Use message queues and background jobs for tasks that don't need to be processed in real-time.

Remember, scalability isn't just about handling more load. It's about doing so efficiently and cost-effectively.

Performance: Speed is King

In the world of software, performance is like the elevator in a skyscraper. If it's slow, it doesn't matter how beautiful or well-designed the rest of the building is – people will be frustrated.

Performance considerations should be baked into your design from the start. Here are some key areas to focus on:

1. Efficient Algorithms: Choose the right algorithms for your data structures and operations. An O(n^2) algorithm might work fine for small datasets but could bring your system to its knees as data grows.
2. Database Optimization: Design your database schema and queries with performance in mind. Use indexes judiciously, optimize your queries, and consider denormalization where appropriate.
3. Caching: Implement caching at various levels – database queries, API responses, and even full page caching for static content.
4. Lazy Loading: Don't load everything at once. Load data and perform computations only when they're needed.

5. Concurrency: Design your system to handle multiple operations concurrently where possible.

We improved the performance of a slow API by implementing a smart caching strategy and optimizing our database queries. The response time went from several seconds to milliseconds, and our users were thrilled!

Security: Fortifying Your Castle

In today's digital landscape, security isn't just a feature – it's a necessity. You wouldn't build a house without locks on the doors, would you? Similarly, security should be a fundamental part of your solution design.

Here are some key security considerations:

1. Authentication and Authorization: Implement robust systems to verify user identities and control access to resources.
2. Data Encryption: Encrypt sensitive data both in transit and at rest.
3. Input Validation: Never trust user input. Validate and sanitize all input to prevent injection attacks.
4. Principle of Least Privilege: Give users and processes only the permissions they absolutely need.
5. Regular Updates and Patch Management: Design your system to allow for easy updates and patching of security vulnerabilities.
6. Logging and Monitoring: Implement comprehensive logging and monitoring to detect and respond to security incidents.

We can implement multi-factor authentication, end-to-end encryption, and a comprehensive audit logging system. It was like building a digital fortress!

Maintainability: Preparing for Change

The only constant in software development is change. Your solution design should embrace this reality and make future modifications as painless as possible.

Here are some maintainability considerations:

1. Modularity: Design your system as a collection of loosely coupled modules. This makes it easier to update or replace individual components without affecting the entire system.

2. Clean Code Practices: Follow clean code principles like SOLID. Write code that's easy to read, understand, and modify.
3. Documentation: Maintain comprehensive documentation, including code comments, API docs, and architecture diagrams.
4. Automated Testing: Design with testability in mind. Implement unit tests, integration tests, and end-to-end tests to catch regressions early.
5. Configuration Management: Externalize configuration settings to make it easy to modify system behavior without code changes.

With poor maintainability led to a complete rewrite after just a few years. On the flip side, I've worked on systems that have evolved gracefully over a decade thanks to good maintainability practices.

Interoperability: Playing Well with Others

In today's interconnected world, your software rarely exists in isolation. It needs to play well with other systems, both internal and external. This is where interoperability comes in.

Key interoperability considerations include:

1. Standard Protocols: Use widely accepted protocols like REST or GraphQL for APIs.
2. Data Formats: Choose standard data formats like JSON or XML for data exchange.
3. API Design: Design clear, well-documented APIs that are easy for other systems to consume.
4. Versioning: Implement API versioning to allow for changes without breaking existing integrations.
5. Error Handling: Provide clear, informative error messages to help integrate with your system.

If we had to integrate with a dozen different third-party systems. Our focus on interoperability made this complex task manageable and allowed for seamless communication between systems.

Documentation and Modeling Techniques: Communicating Your Vision

Now that we've covered the key design considerations, let's talk about how to effectively communicate your design to stakeholders, team members, and even your future self. This is where documentation and modeling techniques come into play.

UML Diagrams: The Universal Language of Software Design

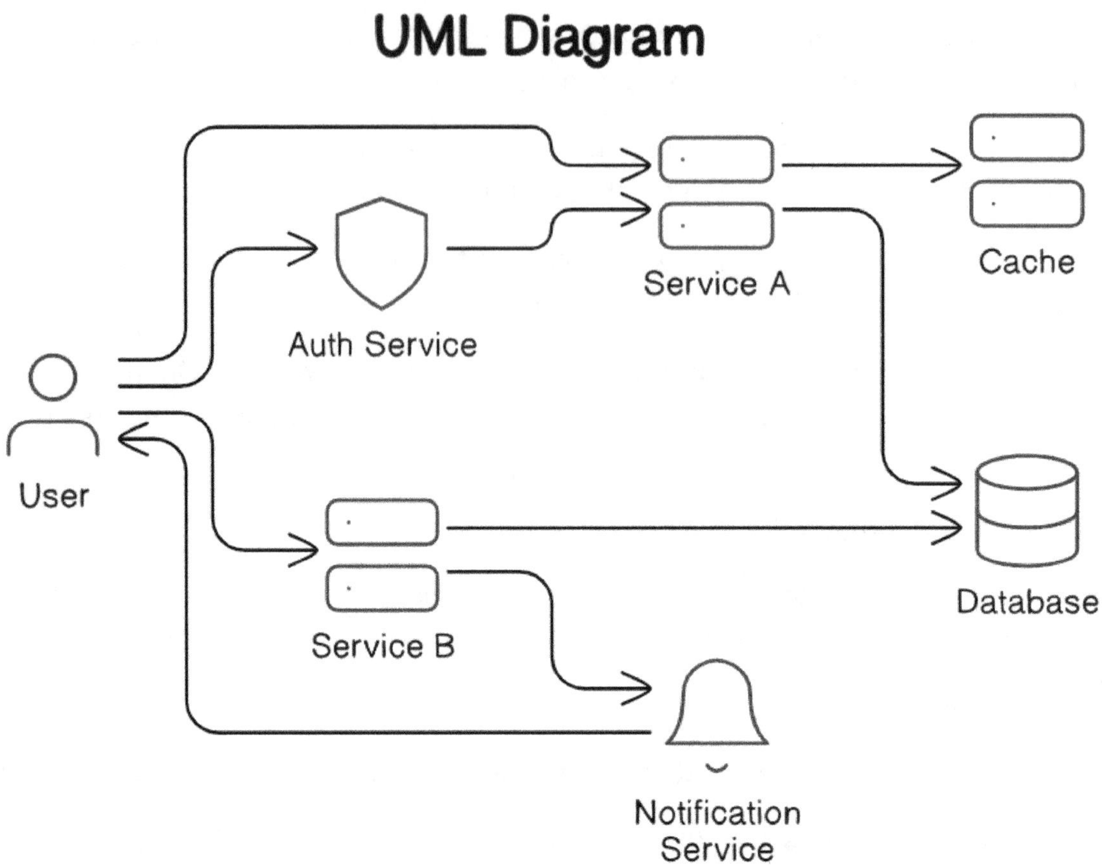

Unified Modeling Language (UML) diagrams are like the blueprints of software design. They provide a standardized way to visualize the design of a system.

Here are some key UML diagrams you should be familiar with:

1. Class Diagrams: These show the static structure of the system, including classes, their attributes, methods, and relationships between classes.
2. Sequence Diagrams: These illustrate how objects interact with each other over time. They're great for showing the flow of control in use cases.
3. Activity Diagrams: These represent the workflow or business processes in your system. They're like flowcharts on steroids.
4. Component Diagrams: These show how different components of your system are organized and how they depend on each other.

5. Deployment Diagrams: These illustrate the physical deployment of artifacts to nodes. They're useful for showing how your software will be distributed across hardware.

UML diagrams serve as a universal language for distributed teams, enabling clear communication of complex design concepts across different time zones. This visual approach bridges geographical gaps and aligns team members on system architecture.

Architecture Decision Records (ADRs): Documenting Your Choices

Architecture Decision Records are a great way to document important architectural decisions, including the context, the decision made, and the consequences of that decision.

An ADR typically includes:

1. Title: A short phrase describing the decision.
2. Status: Proposed, accepted, rejected, deprecated, superseded, etc.
3. Context: The forces at play and the problem you're trying to solve.
4. Decision: The change you're proposing or have made.
5. Consequences: What becomes easier or more difficult because of this change.

ADRs (Architecture Decision Records) prove invaluable for onboarding and historical context, clearly documenting the rationale behind design choices. They eliminate ambiguity when revisiting past decisions, answering the critical question: *"Why was this approach chosen?"*

Data Flow Diagrams: Tracking the Journey of Data

Data Flow Diagrams (DFDs) are excellent tools for visualizing how data moves through your system. They show the inputs, outputs, storage points, and routes between each destination.

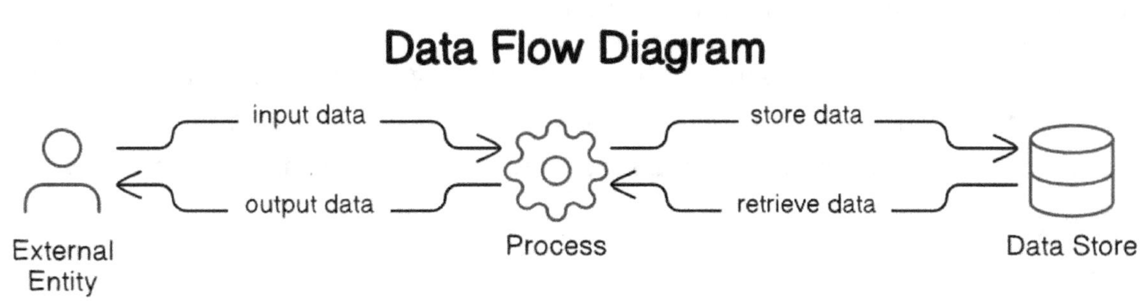

A typical DFD includes:

1. External Entities: Sources or destinations of data outside the system.
2. Processes: Activities that transform data.
3. Data Stores: Places where data is held.
4. Data Flows: Routes that data takes between entities, processes, and stores.

Data Flow Diagrams (DFDs) can create clarity in complex systems by visually mapping how information moves through processes. Stakeholders often experience breakthrough understanding when seeing their system's data flows visualized, revealing previously opaque interactions.

API Documentation: Your System's User Manual

If your system's APIs are its public interface, then API documentation is its user manual. Good API documentation can make the difference between developers loving or hating your system.

Key elements of good API documentation include:

1. Clear descriptions of each endpoint
2. Request and response formats
3. Authentication methods
4. Error codes and their meanings
5. Example requests and responses
6. Rate limiting information

Tools like Swagger (OpenAPI) can help you create interactive API documentation that developers can use to understand and even test your APIs.

Outdated or incomplete API documentation creates significant integration challenges, similar to assembling furniture with missing instructions. Prioritizing comprehensive and up-to-date documentation dramatically reduces integration issues and decreases support requests.

Architecture Diagrams: The Big Picture

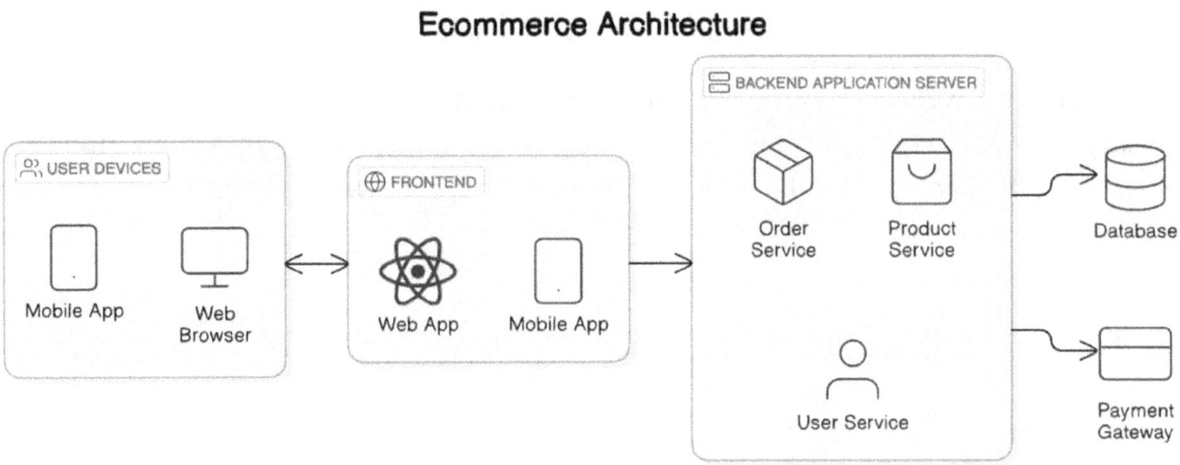

While UML diagrams are great for detailed design, sometimes you need to step back and show the big picture. This is where architecture diagrams come in.

An architecture diagram typically shows:

1. Major components of the system
2. How these components interact
3. External systems and integrations
4. Data stores
5. User interfaces

We can use architecture diagrams in discussions with stakeholders who may not be interested in the technical details but need to understand the overall structure of the system.

Conclusion: Bringing It All Together

Designing a software solution is a complex task that requires careful consideration of various factors. From choosing the right architectural style to ensuring your system is scalable, performant, and secure, there's a lot to think about. And once you've made all these decisions, communicating them effectively through documentation and modeling is crucial.

Remember, good design is iterative. Don't expect to get everything perfect on the first try. Be prepared to revisit and refine your design as you learn more about the problem domain and as requirements evolve.

Chapter 5: Principles of Solution Design

As we wrap up this chapter, I want to leave you with one final thought: design is not just about solving today's problems but about creating a foundation that can adapt to tomorrow's challenges. So, dream big, plan carefully, and build flexibly.

In the next chapter, we'll dive deeper into high-level design, focusing on system architecture. We'll explore how to break down your system into components, model data flows, and select the right technology stack. So, keep your architect's hat on – we're about to start bringing your design to life!

Chapter 6: High-Level Design: System Architecture

Introduction: The Blueprint of Your Software

Picture this: you're about to build your dream house. You wouldn't just start laying bricks without a plan, would you? Of course not! You'd start with a blueprint – a high-level design that outlines the overall structure, the layout of rooms, and how everything fits together. Well, my friend, that's exactly what we're doing in this chapter, but for software.

Welcome to the exciting world of high-level design and system architecture! This is where we take the requirements we've gathered and start shaping them into a tangible structure for our software. It's like being an architect, but instead of buildings, we're designing digital systems.

System architecture for large projects can initially seem overwhelming—like solving a giant puzzle without seeing the full picture. The key is breaking it down into manageable components and clearly visualizing their interactions, which is exactly what this chapter will demonstrate.

Component Identification and Interaction

Breaking Down the Big Picture

Let's start by identifying the main components of our system. Think of these as the rooms in our software house. Each component has a specific purpose and function, just like how a kitchen is for cooking and a bedroom is for sleeping.

To identify components, ask yourself:

1. What are the major functionalities of the system?
2. Can these functionalities be grouped logically?
3. What data or services does each group need to provide or consume?

For example, if we're designing an e-commerce system, we might identify components like:

- User Management
- Product Catalog
- Shopping Cart
- Order Processing
- Payment Gateway
- Inventory Management

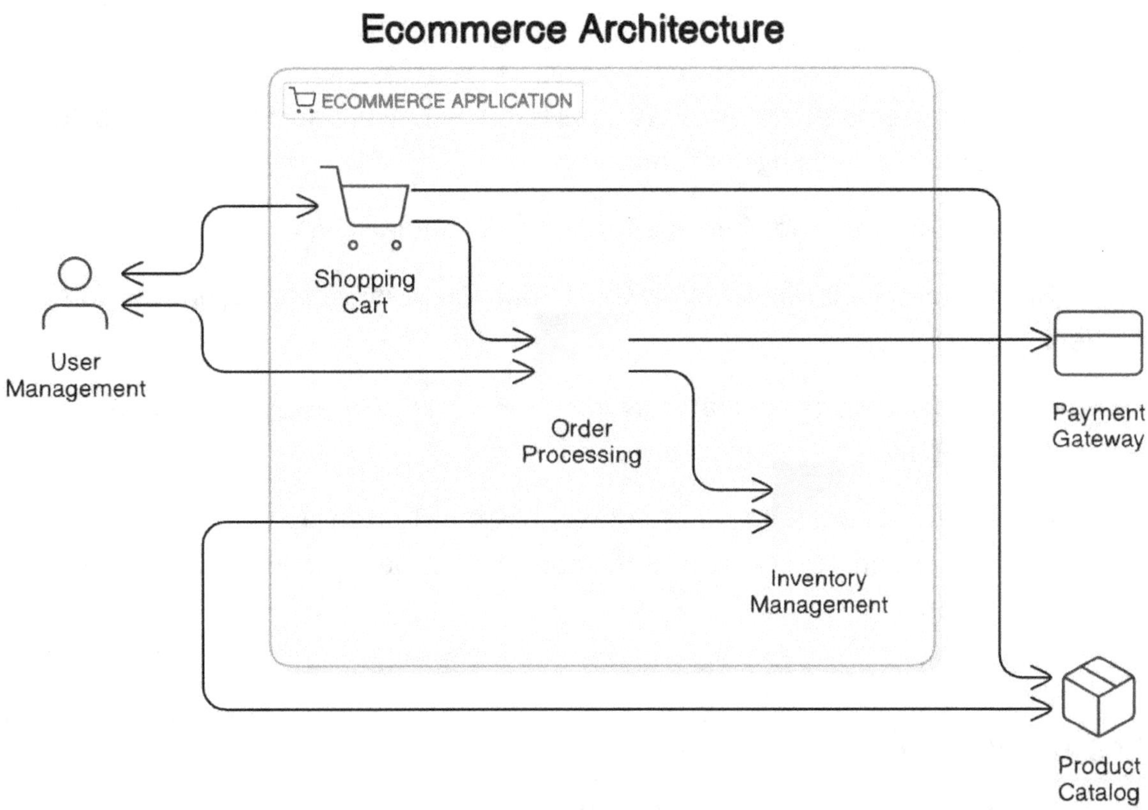

Each of these components encapsulates a specific set of related functions and data.

Making Connections: Component Interactions

Now that we've identified our components, it's time to figure out how they talk to each other. This is crucial because no component exists in isolation – they need to work together to create a functioning system.

Think about the interactions between components as the doorways and hallways in our house. How does someone move from the kitchen to the living room? In software terms, how does data flow from the Product Catalog to the Shopping Cart?

Here's how you can approach this:

1. For each component, list out what information it needs and what information it provides.
2. Identify which components need to communicate directly.
3. Determine the nature of these communications (e.g., synchronous, asynchronous, event-driven).

Let's use our e-commerce example:

- The User Management component needs to provide user information to the Shopping Cart and Order Processing components.
- The Product Catalog feeds information to the Shopping Cart.
- The Shopping Cart interacts with the Order Processing component when a user checks out.
- Order Processing communicates with the Payment Gateway for transactions and Inventory Management to update stock levels.

Visualizing these interactions can be incredibly helpful. I often use diagrams to map out these relationships. It's amazing how much clearer things become when you can see them laid out in front of you.

Data Flow and Process Modeling

Charting the Course of Data

Now that we know how our components interact, let's dive deeper into how data flows through our system. This is where we start to see our software come to life!

Data flow diagrams (DFDs) are fantastic tools for this. They show how data moves between different processes and external entities. I like to think of it as tracking the journey of a drop of water through a river system – where does it come from, where does it go, and how does it change along the way?

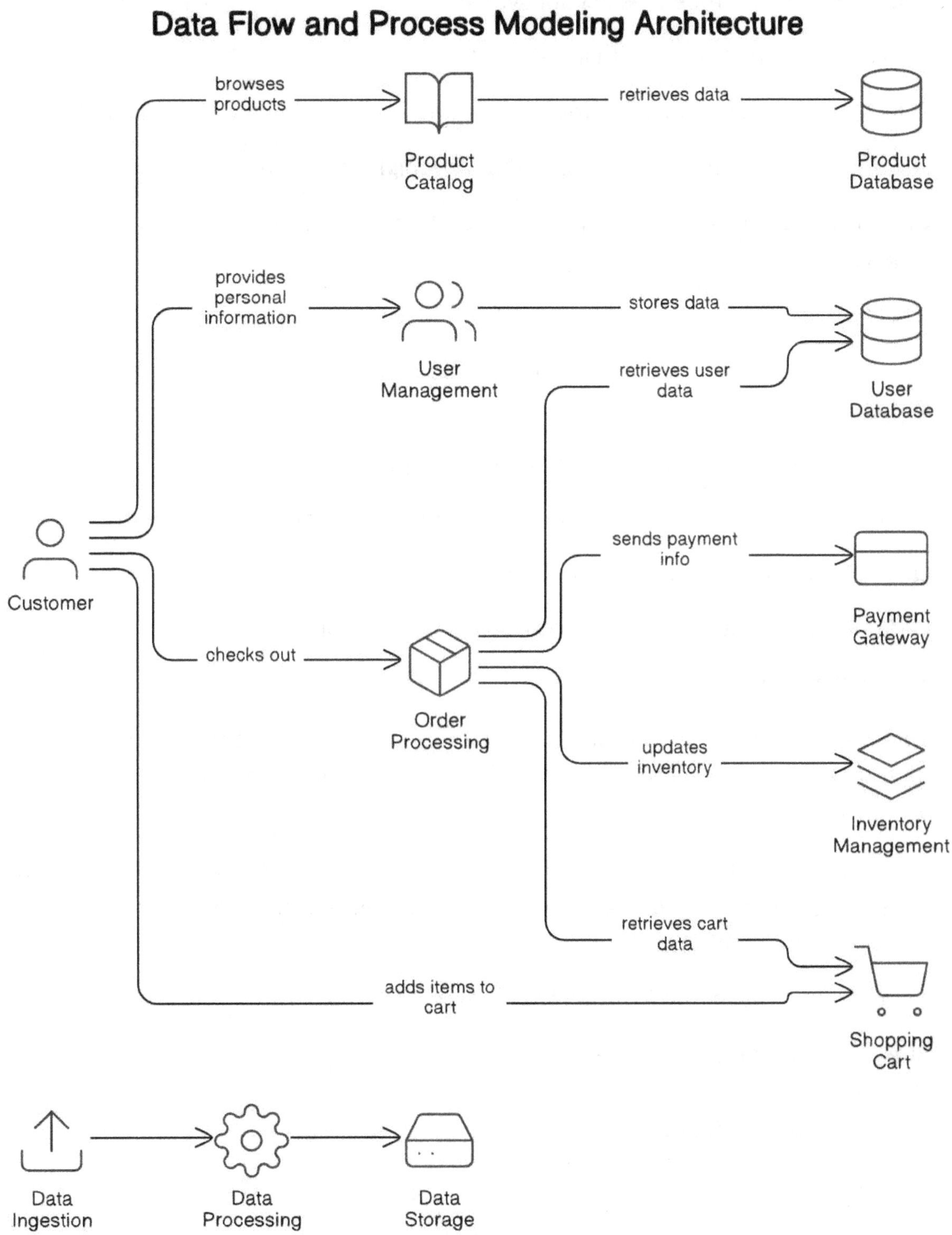

Here's how you can create a basic data flow diagram:

1. Identify external entities (sources and destinations of data outside your system).

2. List out the main processes in your system.
3. Show data stores (where data is held).
4. Draw arrows to represent the flow of data between entities, processes, and stores.

For our e-commerce system, a simplified data flow might look like this:

1. Customer (external entity) provides personal information → User Management process
2. User Management stores data → User Database (data store)
3. Customer browses products → Product Catalog process retrieves data from Product Database
4. Customer adds items to cart → Shopping Cart process
5. Customer checks out → Order Processing retrieves cart data and user data
6. Order Processing sends payment info → Payment Gateway (external entity)
7. Order Processing updates → Inventory Management process

Modeling the Process

While data flow diagrams show us the movement of data, process models help us understand the sequence of activities in our system. Think of this as the recipe for how our system operates.

One popular method for process modeling is the Business Process Model and Notation (BPMN). It's like creating a flowchart, but with standardized symbols that represent different types of activities and decisions.

Here's a simple process model for placing an order:

1. Start → Customer logs in
2. Customer searches for product
3. Decision: Product found?
    - Yes → Customer adds to cart
    - No → Return to search
4. Customer proceeds to checkout
5. System validates order
6. Decision: Order valid?
    - Yes → Process payment
    - No → Return to cart

Chapter 6: High-Level Design: System Architecture

7. Decision: Payment successful?
   - Yes → Confirm order
   - No → Display error message
8. End

Order Placement Process

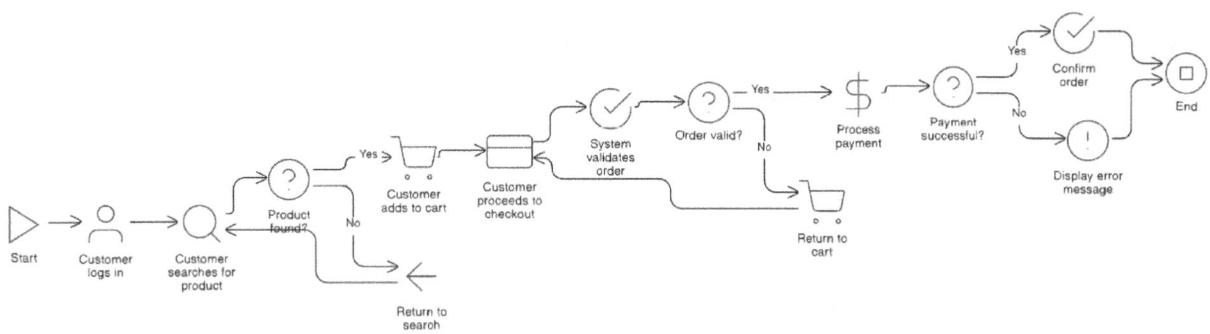

Creating these models helps you identify potential bottlenecks, error points, and opportunities for optimization. I've lost count of how many times these diagrams have helped me spot issues before a single line of code was written!

Technology Stack Selection

Choosing Your Tools

Alright, now we're getting to the fun part – picking our technology stack! This is where we decide what tools and technologies we'll use to build our system. It's like choosing the materials for our house. Do we want brick, wood, or steel? Each has its pros and cons.

Selecting the right technology stack is crucial. It can impact everything from development speed to scalability and maintenance. Here are some factors to consider:

1. Project requirements: What does your system need to do?
2. Scalability: How much growth do you anticipate?
3. Performance: What are the speed and efficiency requirements?
4. Team expertise: What technologies is your team familiar with?
5. Community and support: How active is the community? Is there good documentation?
6. Cost: What's your budget for licenses, hosting, etc.?

Let's break down a typical technology stack:

1. Front-end: This is what the user interacts with. Popular choices include:
    - React.js
    - Angular
    - Vue.js
2. Back-end: This is where the business logic lives. Options include:
    - Node.js with Express
    - Python with Django or Flask
    - Java with Spring Boot
    - C# with .NET Core
3. Database: Where we store our data. Consider:
    - Relational databases like PostgreSQL or MySQL
    - NoSQL databases like MongoDB or Cassandra
4. Caching: For improved performance. Options include:
    - Redis
    - Memcached
5. Message Queues: For handling asynchronous processes:
    - RabbitMQ
    - Apache Kafka
6. Cloud Services: For hosting and additional services:
    - AWS
    - Google Cloud Platform
    - Microsoft Azure

Remember, there's no one-size-fits-all solution. The best stack for you depends on your specific needs and constraints.

Selecting a full-stack JavaScript framework initially appeared efficient—offering a unified language for development. However, as the project scaled, its limitations in handling data-intensive tasks became apparent, necessitating a refactor to Python for backend processing. This highlights the importance of regularly reassessing technology choices to align with evolving project requirements.

Putting It All Together: Creating Your System Architecture

Now that we've identified our components, mapped out their interactions, modeled our data flow and processes, and selected our technology stack, it's time to bring it all together into a cohesive system architecture.

Your system architecture is like the master plan for your software house. It shows how all the pieces fit together and provides a high-level view of your entire system.

Here's how you can approach creating your system architecture:

1. Start with a high-level diagram showing your main components and their interactions.
2. Layer in your technology stack, showing which technologies will be used for each component.
3. Include your data stores and how they connect to various components.
4. Show external systems or APIs that your system will interact with.
5. Indicate the main data flows between components.

For our e-commerce example, our system architecture might look something like this:

E-commerce Platform High-Level Architecture

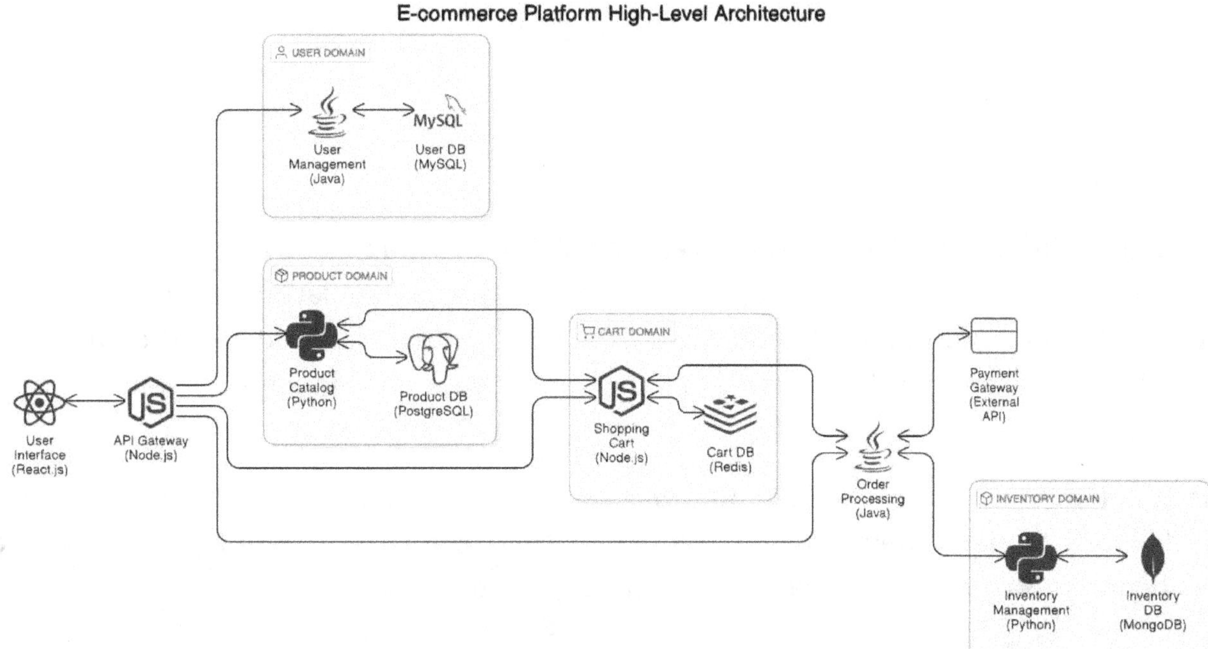

This diagram gives us a clear picture of how our system is structured, what technologies we're using, and how data flows between components.

Conclusion: Your Blueprint for Success

And there you have it! We've journeyed through the exciting world of high-level design and system architecture. We've learned how to break down our system into components, map out their interactions, model our data flows and processes, choose our technology stack, and bring it all together into a comprehensive system architecture.

Remember, this high-level design is your blueprint for success. It guides your development process, helps communicate your vision to stakeholders, and provides a reference point as you dive into the more detailed aspects of your system design.

As you move forward, keep in mind that system architecture is not set in stone. As you progress through development, you may discover new requirements or challenges that require adjustments to your design. That's perfectly normal! The key is to start with a solid foundation and be prepared to iterate and evolve your design as needed.

In our next chapter, we'll dive deeper into the details of each component, exploring low-level design and detailed component specifications. But for now, take a moment to appreciate the big picture you've created. You're well on your way to building a robust, scalable, and efficient software system!

Chapter 7: Low-Level Design: Detailed Component Specifications

Introduction

Welcome to the exciting world of low-level design! If you've made it this far in your software development journey, you're about to dive into one of the most crucial and rewarding phases of the entire process. In this chapter, we'll explore the intricacies of detailed component specifications, where we'll transform high-level concepts into concrete, implementable designs.

Transitioning from high-level design to low-level implementation can be both exhilarating and daunting for developers. The process of transforming abstract concepts into concrete specifications is a critical skill we'll explore in this journey.

The Importance of Low-Level Design

Before we roll up our sleeves and get into the nitty-gritty, let's talk about why low-level design is so crucial. You might be thinking, "Can't we just start coding already?" Trust me, I've been there. But skipping this step is like trying to build a house without a blueprint – you might end up with a structure, but it's likely to be unstable and full of issues.

Low-level design serves as your roadmap for implementation. It bridges the gap between the high-level architecture and the actual code. When done right, it can:

1. Reduce development time and costs
2. Improve code quality and maintainability
3. Facilitate better collaboration among team members
4. Make testing and debugging more straightforward

Think of it as creating a detailed recipe for your favorite dish. The high-level design tells you what meal you're making, but the low-level design specifies exactly how much of each ingredient to use and the precise steps to follow.

Class and Object Design

Understanding Classes and Objects

At the heart of low-level design in object-oriented programming lies class and object design. If you're new to these concepts, think of a class as a blueprint and an object as a specific instance created from that blueprint.

Let's use a real-world example. Imagine we're designing a library management system. We might have a class called Book. This class would define the properties (attributes) and behaviors (methods) that all books in our system should have.

```
public class Book {
  private String title;
  private String author;
  private String ISBN;
  private boolean isAvailable;
  public Book(String title, String author, String ISBN) {
    this.title = title;
    this.author = author;
    this.ISBN = ISBN;
    this.isAvailable = true;
```

```
  }
  public void checkout() {
    this.isAvailable = false;
  }
  public void returnBook() {
    this.isAvailable = true;
  }
  // Getters and setters...
}
```

In this example, Book is our class. It has properties like title, author, and ISBN, and methods like checkout() and returnBook(). An object would be a specific book created from this class, like "To Kill a Mockingbird" by Harper Lee.

Designing Effective Classes

When designing classes, keep these principles in mind:

1. **Single Responsibility Principle**: A class should have one, and only one, reason to change. In our Book class, its responsibility is to represent and manage the state of a book.
2. **Encapsulation**: Hide internal details and provide a public interface. Notice how our Book class uses private fields and public methods to control access.
3. **Cohesion**: Methods and properties in a class should be closely related. Our Book class only contains book-related attributes and operations.
4. **Loose Coupling**: Minimize dependencies between classes. We'll explore this more when we discuss relationships between classes.

Relationships Between Classes

In the real world, entities don't exist in isolation, and neither should our classes. There are several types of relationships we can establish between classes:

1. **Association**: A general relationship between classes. For example, a Library class might have an association with the Book class.
2. **Aggregation**: A "has-a" relationship where one class contains another, but the contained class can exist independently. A Shelf might contain Books, but Books can exist without a Shelf.

3. **Composition**: A stronger "has-a" relationship where the contained class cannot exist without the container. For instance, a Library might be composed of Sections. If the Library is destroyed, its Sections cease to exist.

4. **Inheritance**: An "is-a" relationship where one class (subclass) inherits properties and methods from another (superclass). We might have an EBook class that inherits from Book but adds properties like fileSize.

Here's how we might represent some of these relationships in our library system:

```
public class Library {
  private List<Book> books;
  private List<Section> sections;
  // Methods...
}
public class Section {
  private String name;
  private List<Shelf> shelves;
  // Methods...
}
public class Shelf {
  private List<Book> books;
  // Methods...
}
public class EBook extends Book {
  private double fileSize;
  // Additional methods...
}
```

Remember, the key to good class design is to model your system as closely as possible to the real-world domain it represents. This makes your code more intuitive and easier to understand and maintain.

Database Schema Design

Now that we've covered class and object design, let's dive into another crucial aspect of low-level design: database schema design. If classes are the blueprints for your objects in memory, think of database schemas as the blueprints for how your data is organized and stored persistently.

Understanding Database Schemas

A database schema is a structure that defines how data is organized in a database. It includes:

1. Tables (or collections in NoSQL databases)
2. Fields (or attributes) within those tables
3. Relationships between tables
4. Constraints on the data

Let's continue with our library management system example. We'll design a simple relational database schema for it.

Designing Tables

First, we need to identify the main entities in our system. From our previous discussion, we know we have:

1. Books
2. Libraries
3. Sections
4. Shelves

Let's start with the Books table:

```
CREATE TABLE Books (
  BookID INT PRIMARY KEY,
  Title VARCHAR(255) NOT NULL,
  Author VARCHAR(255) NOT NULL,
  ISBN VARCHAR(13) UNIQUE NOT NULL,
  IsAvailable BOOLEAN DEFAULT TRUE
);
```

Notice how this table closely mirrors our Book class. The BookID is our primary key, which uniquely identifies each book. We've also added a UNIQUE constraint to the ISBN to ensure no duplicate ISBNs are entered.

Now, let's create the Libraries table:

```
CREATE TABLE Libraries (
```

```
    LibraryID INT PRIMARY KEY,
    Name VARCHAR(255) NOT NULL,
    Address VARCHAR(255) NOT NULL
);
```

Establishing Relationships

In a relational database, we use foreign keys to establish relationships between tables. Let's create a Sections table that relates to Libraries:

```
CREATE TABLE Sections (
    SectionID INT PRIMARY KEY,
    Name VARCHAR(255) NOT NULL,
    LibraryID INT,
    FOREIGN KEY (LibraryID) REFERENCES Libraries(LibraryID)
);
```

Here, LibraryID in the Sections table is a foreign key that references the LibraryID in the Libraries table. This establishes a one-to-many relationship: one library can have many sections.

Similarly, let's create a Shelves table:

```
CREATE TABLE Shelves (
    ShelfID INT PRIMARY KEY,
    SectionID INT,
    FOREIGN KEY (SectionID) REFERENCES Sections(SectionID)
);
```

Finally, we need a way to associate books with shelves. We could add a ShelfID to the Books table, but what if a book can be on multiple shelves? In this case, we need a junction table:

```
CREATE TABLE BookShelf (
    BookID INT,
    ShelfID INT,
    PRIMARY KEY (BookID, ShelfID),
    FOREIGN KEY (BookID) REFERENCES Books(BookID),
    FOREIGN KEY (ShelfID) REFERENCES Shelves(ShelfID)
);
```

Chapter 7: Low-Level Design: Detailed Component Specifications

This table allows for a many-to-many relationship between books and shelves.

Normalization and Denormalization

When designing database schemas, you'll often hear about normalization and denormalization. Normalization is the process of organizing data to reduce redundancy and improve data integrity. It involves breaking down tables into smaller, more focused tables and using relationships to connect them.

Our schema above is fairly normalized. For example, we don't store the library name in the Sections table; instead, we use a foreign key to reference the Libraries table.

Denormalization, on the other hand, is the process of adding redundant data to improve read performance. You might do this if you find that certain queries are too slow due to the need to join multiple tables.

For instance, if we frequently need to display books with their shelf and section information, we might denormalize our schema by adding SectionName and ShelfID directly to the Books table:

```
ALTER TABLE Books
ADD COLUMN SectionName VARCHAR(255),
ADD COLUMN ShelfID INT;
```

This would speed up these queries but at the cost of data redundancy and potentially more complex update operations.

Considerations for NoSQL Databases

While we've focused on relational database design here, it's worth noting that NoSQL databases often require a different approach. In document databases like MongoDB, for example, you might embed related data within a single document rather than using separate tables with foreign key relationships.

Here's how our Book document might look in MongoDB:

```
{
  "_id": ObjectId("..."),
  "title": "To Kill a Mockingbird",
  "author": "Harper Lee",
  "ISBN": "9780446310789",
  "isAvailable": true,
  "shelf": {
    "id": 1,
```

```
    "section": {
     "id": 1,
     "name": "Fiction",
     "library": {
      "id": 1,
      "name": "Central Library"
     }
    }
   }
  }
```

This approach can lead to faster reads for this specific book's information but may result in data duplication and more complex updates.

The choice between SQL and NoSQL, and the specific design within each, depends on your application's particular needs, expected query patterns, and scaling requirements.

API and Interface Design

The final piece of our low-level design puzzle is API and interface design. This is where we define how our components will communicate with each other and with the outside world. Good API design is crucial for creating maintainable, scalable systems.

Understanding APIs and Interfaces

An Application Programming Interface (API) is a set of protocols, routines, and tools for building software applications. It specifies how software components should interact. An interface, in object-oriented programming, is a contract that specifies the methods a class must implement.

In our library management system, we might have several APIs:

1. A public API for library patrons to search for and reserve books
2. An internal API for librarians to manage books, shelves, and sections
3. An admin API for system management tasks

Let's focus on designing the public API for our library system.

RESTful API Design

One popular approach to API design is REST (Representational State Transfer). RESTful APIs use HTTP methods to perform operations on resources. Here's how we might design a RESTful API for our library system:

1. **Search for books**:

```
GET /api/books?query=mockingbird
```

2. **Get details of a specific book**:

```
GET /api/books/{bookId}
```

3. **Reserve a book**:

```
POST /api/reservations
Body: { "bookId": 123, "userId": 456 }
```

4. **Cancel a reservation**:

```
DELETE /api/reservations/{reservationId}
```

5. **Get user's current reservations**:

```
GET /api/users/{userId}/reservations
```

API Documentation

Clear, comprehensive documentation is crucial for any API. Here's an example of how you might document the "Get details of a specific book" endpoint:

```
GET /api/books/{bookId}

Description: Retrieves detailed information about a specific book.

Path Parameters:
 - bookId: The unique identifier of the book (integer)

Response:
 200 OK:
  {
   "id": 123,
   "title": "To Kill a Mockingbird",
   "author": "Harper Lee",
   "ISBN": "9780446310789",
   "isAvailable": true,
   "currentShelf": {
    "id": 45,
    "section": {
     "id": 12,
     "name": "Fiction"
```

```
            }
        }
    }

404 Not Found:
    {
      "error": "Book not found"
    }
```

Interface Design in Object-Oriented Programming

In the context of our Java classes, we might define interfaces to ensure consistent behavior across different types of library items. For example:

```
public interface LibraryItem {
    String getTitle();
    String getAuthor();
    String getUniqueIdentifier();
    boolean isAvailable();
    void checkout();
    void returnItem();
}

public class Book implements LibraryItem {
    // Implementation of LibraryItem methods
}

public class EBook implements LibraryItem {
    // Implementation of LibraryItem methods
}
```

This interface ensures that all library items, whether physical books or ebooks, have a consistent set of methods that can be called.

Designing for Extensibility

When designing APIs and interfaces, always keep extensibility in mind. You want your design to be flexible enough to accommodate future changes without breaking existing functionality.

For example, in our RESTful API, we might version our endpoints:

```
GET /api/v1/books/{bookId}
```

This allows us to introduce a new version (v2) in the future if we need to make breaking changes, while still supporting the old version for existing clients.

Similarly, in our Java interface design, we might use the Interface Segregation Principle (part of the SOLID principles) to create smaller, more focused interfaces:

```
public interface Readable {
  String getTitle();
  String getAuthor();
}

public interface Borrowable {
  boolean isAvailable();
  void checkout();
  void returnItem();
}

public interface LibraryItem extends Readable, Borrowable {
  String getUniqueIdentifier();
}
```

This approach allows for more flexibility. For instance, if we later introduce non-borrowable reference materials, they could implement Readable without needing to implement Borrowable.

Error Handling and Edge Cases

A crucial part of API and interface design is considering how to handle errors and edge cases. In our RESTful API, we should define standard error responses:

```
{
 "error": {
  "code": "BOOK_NOT_FOUND",
  "message": "The requested book could not be found",
  "details": {
   "bookId": 123
  }
 }
}
```

For our Java interfaces, we should consider throwing appropriate exceptions:

```
public interface LibraryItem {
    // ...other methods...

    void checkout() throws ItemNotAvailableException;
}
```

Performance Considerations

When designing APIs, also consider performance implications. For instance, in our book search API, we might want to allow for pagination to avoid returning too much data at once:

```
GET /api/books?query=mockingbird&page=1&pageSize=20
```

In our Java interfaces, we might include methods that allow for batch operations:

```
public interface LibraryItemRepository {
    List<LibraryItem> findByIds(List<String> ids);
    void checkoutMultiple(List<String> ids) throws ItemNotAvailableException;
}
```

These batch operations can significantly improve performance when dealing with multiple items.

Conclusion

Low-level design is where the rubber meets the road in software development. It's where we transform abstract concepts into concrete, implementable specifications. By carefully designing our classes and objects, crafting efficient database schemas, and creating clear, extensible APIs and interfaces, we lay the foundation for a robust, maintainable system.

Remember, good low-level design is an iterative process. Don't be afraid to revisit and refine your designs as you gain more insight into your system's requirements and behavior. And always keep the end-users of your designs in mind – whether they're other developers, database administrators, or API consumers.

As we wrap up this chapter, take a moment to reflect on how these low-level design concepts apply to your current or future projects. How might you use class and object design to better model your problem domain? Could your database schema be optimized for your most common queries? Are your APIs intuitive and easy to use?

Chapter 7: Low-Level Design: Detailed Component Specifications

In the next chapter, we'll explore how to turn these detailed specifications into actual code, diving into development best practices that will help bring your designs to life. But for now, pat yourself on the back – you've just completed one of the most crucial stages in the software development life cycle!

Chapter 8: Development Best Practices

Introduction

Welcome to the heart of software development! If you've made it this far, you've already navigated through the initial stages of the Software Development Life Cycle (SDLC). You've gathered requirements, conducted feasibility studies, and designed your solution. Now, it's time to roll up your sleeves and dive into the actual development process.

But hold on a second! Before you start furiously typing away at your keyboard, let's talk about some development best practices that can make your life (and your team's life) a whole lot easier. Trust me, I've learned these lessons the hard way, and I'm here to help you avoid the same pitfalls.

In this chapter, we'll explore three crucial aspects of development best practices: coding standards and guidelines, version control and collaboration tools, and code review processes. By the end of this chapter, you'll have a solid foundation for writing clean, maintainable code and collaborating effectively with your team.

Coding Standards and Guidelines

The Importance of Consistency

Have you ever opened up a codebase and felt like you were reading a mishmash of different programming styles? It's like walking into a room where everyone is speaking a different dialect of the same language. Sure, you can eventually figure out what's going on, but it takes a lot more time and effort.

That's where coding standards come in. They're like the grammar rules of programming. They ensure that everyone on the team is "speaking" the same dialect, making it easier for developers to read and understand each other's code.

Working without established coding standards leads to inconsistent styles across developers, making codebases difficult to read and maintain. This results in frustration, wasted time, and maintenance challenges—highlighting the critical importance of consistent coding conventions.

Establishing Your Coding Standards

So, how do you establish coding standards for your team? Here are some key areas to consider:

1. **Naming Conventions**: Decide on a consistent way to name variables, functions, classes, and files. For example, you might use camelCase for variables and functions, PascalCase for classes, and kebab-case for file names.
2. **Code Formatting**: Agree on indentation (spaces or tabs?), line length, where to place braces, and how to format control structures.
3. **Comments and Documentation**: Establish guidelines for when and how to write comments, as well as standards for documenting functions, classes, and modules.
4. **Error Handling**: Define how errors should be handled and reported throughout the codebase.
5. **File Organization**: Decide on a consistent structure for organizing files and directories in your project.
6. **Design Patterns**: Agree on which design patterns to use in specific situations to ensure consistency across the codebase.

Here's a simple example of how these standards might look in practice:

```
class UserAccount:
  def __init__(self, username, email):
    self.username = username
    self.email = email
  def update_email(self, new_email):
    """
    Update the user's email address.
    Args:
      new_email (str): The new email address for the user.
    Raises:
      ValueError: If the new email is not valid.
```

```
    """
    if self.is_valid_email(new_email):
        self.email = new_email
    else:
        raise ValueError("Invalid email address")

@staticmethod
def is_valid_email(email):
    # Implementation of email validation
    pass
```

Tools for Enforcing Coding Standards

Now, you might be thinking, "That's all well and good, but how do I make sure everyone actually follows these standards?" Great question! This is where linting tools come in handy.

Linters are tools that analyze your code for potential errors and style violations. They can be integrated into your development environment to provide real-time feedback as you code. Some popular linters include:

- ESLint for JavaScript
- Pylint for Python
- RuboCop for Ruby
- StyleCop for C#

These tools can be configured to enforce your team's specific coding standards, catching style violations before they even make it into your codebase.

Version Control and Collaboration Tools

The Magic of Version Control

Imagine you're writing a novel. You have a brilliant idea for a plot twist, so you rewrite a significant portion of your story. But a week later, you realize that your original idea was better. Without version control, you'd be in trouble. But with version control, you can easily go back to any previous version of your work.

Version control systems (VCS) do the same thing for your code. They allow you to track changes, revert to previous versions, and collaborate with others without stepping on each other's toes.

Git: The King of Version Control

While there are several version control systems out there, Git has emerged as the de facto standard in the software development world. If you're not already using Git, I strongly recommend giving it a try.

Here are some key Git concepts you should be familiar with:

1. **Repositories**: These are like project folders that Git tracks.
2. **Commits**: These are snapshots of your code at a specific point in time.
3. **Branches**: These allow you to work on different versions of your code simultaneously.
4. **Merging**: This is the process of combining changes from different branches.
5. **Pull Requests**: These are requests to merge changes from one branch into another, often used for code review.

Let's walk through a typical Git workflow:

```
# Create a new branch for your feature
git checkout -b new-feature
# Make changes to your code
# ...
# Stage your changes
git add .
# Commit your changes
git commit -m "Implemented new feature"
# Push your changes to the remote repository
git push origin new-feature
# Create a pull request on GitHub or your preferred Git platform
```

Collaboration Tools: Beyond Version Control

While Git is fantastic for version control, there are other tools that can enhance collaboration in your development process. Here are a few I've found particularly useful:

1. **Issue Trackers**: Tools like Jira, Trello, or GitHub Issues help you keep track of tasks, bugs, and feature requests.
2. **Documentation Tools**: Tools like Confluence, Notion, or even a well-organized Wiki can help keep your team's knowledge base up to date.
3. **Communication Tools**: Slack, Microsoft Teams, or Discord can facilitate quick, informal communication among team members.
4. **Continuous Integration/Continuous Deployment (CI/CD) Tools**: Tools like Jenkins, Travis CI, or GitLab CI can automate your build, test, and deployment processes.

Remember, the goal of these tools is to make collaboration easier and more efficient. Don't get bogged down in tool overload – choose the ones that work best for your team and stick with them.

Code Review Processes

The Power of Peer Review

Have you ever had that moment of panic when you realize you've made a silly mistake in your code, and it's already in production? We've all been there. That's where code reviews come in.

Code reviews are like having a friend proofread your essay before you submit it. They provide a second set of eyes to catch errors, improve code quality, and share knowledge among team members.

Establishing a Code Review Process

Here's a step-by-step guide to implementing an effective code review process:

1. **Create a Pull Request**: When a developer completes a feature or bug fix, they create a pull request (PR) in your version control system.
2. **Assign Reviewers**: Assign one or more team members to review the code. It's often helpful to have both a senior developer and a peer review the code.
3. **Review the Code**: Reviewers examine the code for errors, style violations, and potential improvements. They can leave comments directly in the PR.

4. **Discuss and Iterate**: The author and reviewers discuss any issues or suggestions, and the author makes necessary changes.

5. **Approve and Merge**: Once all reviewers are satisfied, they approve the PR, and it can be merged into the main branch.

Code Review Process Workflow

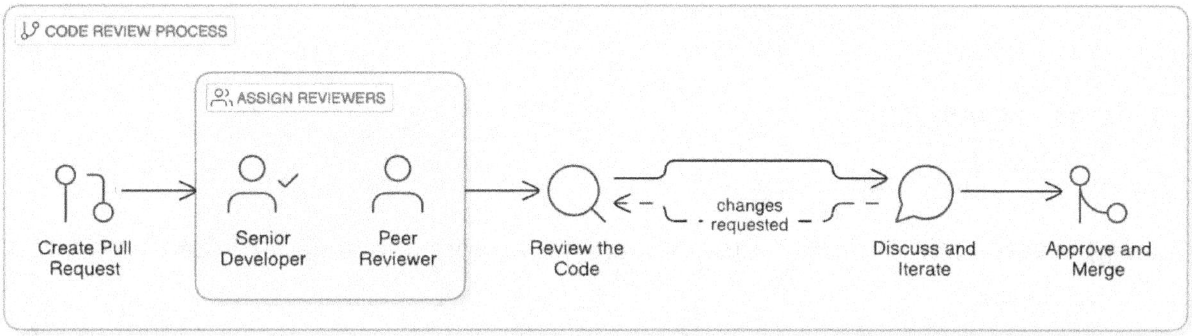

Best Practices for Code Reviews

To get the most out of your code reviews, consider these best practices:

1. **Be Timely**: Try to review code within 24 hours of it being submitted. This keeps the development process moving and prevents large, intimidating PRs from piling up.

2. **Be Specific**: When leaving comments, be as specific as possible. Instead of saying "This could be better," say "Consider using a switch statement here for better readability."

3. **Be Kind**: Remember, you're reviewing code, not the person. Keep your comments constructive and professional.

4. **Look for the Big Picture**: Don't just focus on style issues. Look for architectural problems, performance issues, and security vulnerabilities.

5. **Use Automated Tools**: Use linters and other automated tools to catch style issues and simple errors, freeing up reviewers to focus on more complex issues.

6. **Learn and Share**: Use code reviews as an opportunity to learn from others and share your knowledge.

Here's an example of a constructive code review comment:

```
In the `processPayment` function:
```

Consider breaking this function into smaller, more focused functions. For example, you could have separate functions for validating the payment details, processing the transaction, and updating the user's account. This would improve readability and make the code easier to test.

Also, it might be worth adding some error handling around the API call to the payment processor. What happens if the API is down or returns an error?

The Benefits of Code Reviews

Implementing a robust code review process can have numerous benefits:

1. **Improved Code Quality**: Catching bugs and improving code structure before it hits production.
2. **Knowledge Sharing**: Junior developers can learn from seniors, and everyone can learn about different parts of the codebase.
3. **Consistent Coding Standards**: Reviews help enforce the coding standards we discussed earlier.
4. **Reduced Technical Debt**: Addressing potential issues early prevents them from accumulating into larger problems down the line.
5. **Team Cohesion**: Regular code reviews foster a culture of collaboration and shared ownership of the codebase.

Conclusion

Implementing development best practices might seem like extra work at first, but trust me, it pays off in the long run. Consistent coding standards make your codebase more readable and maintainable. Effective use of version control and collaboration tools streamlines your development process. And a solid code review process catches bugs early and promotes knowledge sharing within your team.

Remember, these practices aren't set in stone. As your team grows and evolves, your practices should too. Regularly revisit and refine your development practices to ensure they're still serving your team effectively.

As we wrap up this chapter on development best practices, we're ready to move on to the next crucial phase of the SDLC: testing. In the next chapter, we'll dive into unit testing strategies, exploring how to ensure your individually developed components work as expected before they're integrated into the larger system. Get ready to embrace the world of test-driven development!

Chapter 9: Unit Testing Strategies

Introduction

Welcome to the world of unit testing! If you've ever felt the frustration of discovering bugs in your code after deployment, or if you've spent countless hours debugging issues that could have been caught earlier, then this chapter is for you. I'm here to guide you through the ins and outs of unit testing strategies, and by the end of this chapter, you'll be equipped with the knowledge and tools to make your code more robust, reliable, and easier to maintain.

As a software developer myself, I've learned the hard way that skipping unit tests or doing them haphazardly can lead to sleepless nights and stressful workdays. But fear not! I'm going to share with you the strategies that have saved me time and time again, and hopefully, they'll do the same for you.

Understanding Unit Testing

Before we dive into the strategies, let's make sure we're on the same page about what unit testing really is.

Unit testing is the practice of testing individual components or units of your code in isolation. These "units" are typically the smallest testable parts of your software, such as functions, methods, or classes. The goal is to validate that each unit of the software performs as designed.

You might be thinking, "But I already test my code when I run it!" And you're right, but unit testing goes a step further. It's about creating automated tests that can be run quickly and repeatedly, catching issues before they make it to production.

The Importance of Unit Testing

Skipping unit testing to meet tight deadlines often backfires, leading to post-deployment bugs that require extensive fixes. This approach ultimately causes team stress, delays, and client dissatisfaction—demonstrating how critical testing is for long-term efficiency.

Unit testing offers several key benefits:

1. **Early Bug Detection**: Catch and fix issues early in the development cycle when they're easier and cheaper to resolve.
2. **Code Quality**: Writing tests often leads to better-designed, more modular code.

3. **Confidence in Changes**: With a good test suite, you can refactor or add new features with confidence, knowing your tests will catch any regressions.
4. **Documentation**: Tests serve as a form of documentation, showing how your code is supposed to work.
5. **Faster Development**: While it might seem counterintuitive, spending time on tests can actually speed up development in the long run by reducing debugging time.

Now that we understand why unit testing is crucial, let's dive into some key strategies.

Test-Driven Development (TDD)

Test-Driven Development, or TDD, is a development process where you write tests before writing the actual code. It might sound backward at first, but trust me, it's a game-changer.

Here's how TDD typically works:

1. Write a failing test for a feature you want to implement.
2. Run the test to see it fail (because the feature doesn't exist yet).
3. Write the minimum amount of code to make the test pass.
4. Run the test again to see it pass.
5. Refactor your code if necessary, ensuring the test still passes.
6. Repeat for the next feature or piece of functionality.

TDD (Test-Driven Development) often meets initial skepticism, but its effectiveness in improving code quality and reducing defects becomes clear through implementation.

Benefits of TDD

1. **Clearer Code**: Writing tests first forces you to think about the interface and behavior of your code before implementation.
2. **Better Design**: TDD often leads to more modular, loosely coupled code because it's easier to test.
3. **Confidence**: With TDD, you know your code works as soon as you write it, reducing the fear of breaking things.
4. **Living Documentation**: Your tests serve as up-to-date documentation of how your code should behave.

TDD Example

Let's say we're building a simple calculator function. Here's how we might approach it with TDD:

1. Write the test:

```
def test_add():
assert add(2, 3) == 5
```

2. Run the test (it fails because add doesn't exist yet).
3. Write the minimum code to make it pass:

```
def add(a, b):
return 5 # Hardcoded for now
```

4. Run the test (it passes).
5. Refactor:

```
def add(a, b):
return a + b
```

6. Run the test again (it still passes).

This is a simplified example, but it illustrates the TDD process. As you practice TDD, you'll find yourself naturally breaking down complex problems into smaller, more manageable pieces.

Mocking and Stubbing Techniques

When unit testing, you often need to isolate the code you're testing from its dependencies. This is where mocking and stubbing come in handy.

Mocking

Mocking involves creating objects that simulate the behavior of real objects. It's useful when you want to test how your code interacts with other parts of the system without actually using those parts.

For example, let's say you have a function that makes an API call. You don't want your tests to actually make that call every time they run. Instead, you can create a mock object that simulates the API response.

Here's an example using Python's unittest.mock:

```
from unittest.mock import Mock

def get_user_data(user_id):

    # In reality, this would make an API call

    api = APIClient()

    return api.get_user(user_id)

def test_get_user_data():

    # Create a mock APIClient

    mock_api = Mock()

    mock_api.get_user.return_value = {"id": 1, "name": "John Doe"}

    # Replace the real APIClient with our mock

    APIClient = mock_api

    result = get_user_data(1)

    assert result == {"id": 1, "name": "John Doe"}

    mock_api.get_user.assert_called_once_with(1)
```

In this example, we're not testing the API itself, but rather how our code interacts with it.

Stubbing

Stubbing is similar to mocking, but typically simpler. A stub provides canned answers to calls made during the test, usually not responding at all to anything outside what's programmed in for the test.

Here's a simple example:

```
def get_current_time():

    # In reality, this would return the current time

    return datetime.now()
```

```
def is_it_lunchtime():
    current_time = get_current_time()
    return 12 <= current_time.hour < 13
def test_is_it_lunchtime():
    # Stub the get_current_time function
    def stub_time():
        return datetime(2023, 1, 1, 12, 30)  # 12:30 PM
    get_current_time = stub_time
    assert is_it_lunchtime() == True
```

In this case, we've stubbed the get_current_time function to always return a specific time, allowing us to test the is_it_lunchtime function without worrying about what time it actually is.

Code Coverage and Quality Metrics

As you write more tests, you'll want to know how much of your code is actually being tested. This is where code coverage comes in.

Code coverage is a measure of how much of your code is executed when your tests run. It's usually expressed as a percentage and can be broken down into different types:

1. **Line Coverage**: The percentage of lines of code that are executed.
2. **Branch Coverage**: The percentage of branches (like if/else statements) that are executed.
3. **Function Coverage**: The percentage of functions that are called.
4. **Statement Coverage**: The percentage of statements that are executed.

While 100% code coverage might seem like the goal, it's not always practical or even desirable. What's more important is meaningful coverage – tests that actually verify the correctness of your code, not just that it runs.

Measuring Code Coverage

There are many tools available for measuring code coverage, depending on your programming language and environment. For Python, for example, you might use the coverage library:

pip install coverage

coverage run -m unittest discover

coverage report -m

This will run your tests and generate a report showing which lines of code were executed and which weren't.

Quality Metrics

Beyond just coverage, there are other metrics you can use to assess the quality of your tests:

1. **Cyclomatic Complexity**: This measures the number of linearly independent paths through your code. Higher complexity often indicates code that's harder to test and maintain.

2. **Assertion Density**: This is the number of assertions per test. While there's no magic number, too few assertions might indicate weak tests, while too many might make tests brittle and hard to maintain.

3. **Test Run Time**: Faster tests are better because they encourage developers to run them more often. If your tests are taking too long to run, it might be time to optimize them or your code.

4. **Mutation Testing**: This involves making small changes to your code (mutations) and seeing if your tests catch them. It's a way to test your tests!

Remember, these metrics are tools to help you improve your testing, not goals in themselves. Use them as guides, but always prioritize writing meaningful, valuable tests over hitting arbitrary numbers.

Best Practices for Unit Testing

Now that we've covered the main strategies and tools, let's talk about some best practices that can help you write better unit tests.

1. Keep Tests Small and Focused

Each test should ideally test one thing. If you find yourself using the word "and" in your test name, it might be a sign that you should split it into multiple tests.

```
# Not so good
def test_user_creation_and_authentication():
    # Test user creation
    # Test user authentication
# Better
def test_user_creation():
    # Test user creation
def test_user_authentication():
    # Test user authentication
```

2. Use Descriptive Test Names

Your test names should clearly describe what they're testing. This makes it easier to understand what's wrong when a test fails.

```
# Not so good
def test_user():
# Better
def test_user_cannot_have_empty_username():
```

3. Follow the Arrange-Act-Assert Pattern

Structure your tests in three parts:

- Arrange: Set up the test conditions
- Act: Perform the action you're testing
- Assert: Check the results

```
def test_add_item_to_cart():
    # Arrange
```

```
    cart = ShoppingCart()
    item = Item("book", 10.99)

    # Act
    cart.add_item(item)

    # Assert
    assert len(cart.items) == 1
    assert cart.total_price == 10.99
```

4. Don't Test Implementation Details

Test the behavior of your code, not how it's implemented. This allows you to refactor your code without having to change your tests.

```
# Not so good (testing implementation)

def test_add_user_to_database():

  user = User("John")

  database.add(user)

  assert len(database._internal_list) == 1


# Better (testing behavior)

def test_add_user_to_database():

  user = User("John")

  database.add(user)

  assert database.get_user("John") == user
```

5. Use Setup and Teardown

If you have common setup or cleanup code for multiple tests, use setup and teardown methods (the exact syntax depends on your testing framework).

```
class TestDatabase(unittest.TestCase):

  def setUp(self):
```

```
        self.db = Database()
        self.db.connect()

    def tearDown(self):
        self.db.disconnect()

    def test_add_user(self):
        # Test adding a user

    def test_remove_user(self):
        # Test removing a user
```

6. Don't Ignore Failed Tests

A failing test is telling you something important. Don't ignore it or delete it just to make your build pass. Figure out why it's failing and fix the underlying issue.

7. Keep Your Tests Fast

Slow tests discourage developers from running them frequently. If your tests are taking too long, consider:

- Mocking slow operations (like database calls or API requests)
- Running tests in parallel
- Separating slow integration tests from fast unit tests

8. Use Parameterized Tests

If you find yourself writing very similar tests with just different input data, consider using parameterized tests. Many testing frameworks provide ways to run the same test with multiple sets of data.

```
@pytest.mark.parametrize("input,expected", [
    (2, 4),
```

```
    (3, 9),
    (4, 16),
    (5, 25),
])
def test_square(input, expected):
    assert square(input) == expected
```

9. Test Edge Cases

Don't just test the happy path. Make sure to test edge cases and error conditions too.

```
def test_divide():
    assert divide(10, 2) == 5
    assert divide(7, 3) == 2.333 (approx)
    assert divide(10, 0) raises ZeroDivisionError
```

10. Refactor Your Tests

Just like your production code, your test code needs maintenance too. Don't be afraid to refactor your tests to make them clearer or more efficient.

Common Pitfalls in Unit Testing

Even with best practices in mind, there are some common pitfalls that developers often fall into when writing unit tests. Let's explore these and how to avoid them.

1. Testing Too Much in One Go

It's tempting to try to test everything about a piece of code in a single test, but this can lead to tests that are hard to understand and maintain.

```
# Not so good
def test_user_registration():
    user = register_user("john@example.com", "password123")
```

```
    assert user.email == "john@example.com"
    assert user.password != "password123"  # Should be hashed
    assert user.is_active == True
    assert user.created_at is not None
    # ... many more assertions

# Better: Split into multiple focused tests
def test_user_registration_sets_email():
    user = register_user("john@example.com", "password123")
    assert user.email == "john@example.com"

def test_user_registration_hashes_password():
    user = register_user("john@example.com", "password123")
    assert user.password != "password123"
    assert user.check_password("password123")

# ... more specific tests
```

2. Ignoring Test Failures

It's easy to fall into the trap of ignoring failing tests, especially when you're under pressure to deliver. But remember, tests are there to catch issues before they become problems in production.

If a test is consistently failing, don't ignore it or mark it to be skipped. Instead, take the time to understand why it's failing and fix the underlying issue. If the test is no longer relevant, remove it entirely rather than leaving it as a skipped test.

3. Testing the Wrong Things

Sometimes we end up testing things that don't really matter, or testing implementation details rather than behavior.

```
# Not so good: Testing implementation details
def test_add_to_cart():
    cart = ShoppingCart()
    cart.add_item("book")
    assert cart._items[-1] == "book"  # Depends on internal implementation

# Better: Testing behavior
def test_add_to_cart():
    cart = ShoppingCart()
    cart.add_item("book")
    assert "book" in cart.get_items()
```

4. Overusing Mocks

While mocks are useful, overusing them can lead to tests that pass but don't reflect reality. Try to use real objects where possible, and only mock what's necessary.

```
# Overusing mocks
def test_process_order():
    mock_cart = Mock()
    mock_payment = Mock()
    mock_shipping = Mock()
    order = process_order(mock_cart, mock_payment, mock_shipping)
    assert order.status == "completed"

# Better: Use real objects where possible
```

```
def test_process_order():
    cart = ShoppingCart()
    cart.add_item("book")
    payment = PaymentProcessor()
    shipping = ShippingCalculator()
    order = process_order(cart, payment, shipping)
    assert order.status == "completed"
```

5. Writing Tests After the Code

While it's better to have tests written after the fact than no tests at all, writing tests after the code often leads to tests that simply confirm what the code does, rather than what it should do. Try to write tests before or while writing the code, as in Test-Driven Development.

6. Hardcoding Expected Values

Hardcoding expected values can make your tests brittle and prone to breaking when small changes are made.

```
# Not so good
def test_calculate_total():
    cart = ShoppingCart()
    cart.add_item(Item("book", 10.99))
    cart.add_item(Item("pen", 1.99))
    assert cart.calculate_total() == 12.98  # Hardcoded value


# Better
def test_calculate_total():
    cart = ShoppingCart()
    book = Item("book", 10.99)
    pen = Item("pen", 1.99)
```

```
    cart.add_item(book)
    cart.add_item(pen)
    assert cart.calculate_total() == book.price + pen.price
```

7. Not Testing Error Conditions

It's easy to focus on testing the happy path and forget about error conditions. Make sure you're testing how your code handles invalid inputs, edge cases, and error conditions.

```
def test_divide():
    assert divide(10, 2) == 5
    assert divide(7, 3) == pytest.approx(2.33, 0.01)
    with pytest.raises(ValueError):
        divide(10, 0)
```

8. Writing Non-Deterministic Tests

Tests that sometimes pass and sometimes fail (often called "flaky" tests) can be a huge headache. Ensure your tests are deterministic by avoiding dependencies on things like the current time or random numbers.

```
# Not so good
def test_is_it_friday():
    assert is_it_friday() == (datetime.now().weekday() == 4)

# Better
@freeze_time("2023-06-02")  # A Friday
def test_is_it_friday():
    assert is_it_friday() == True

@freeze_time("2023-06-03")  # A Saturday
def test_is_it_not_friday():
```

```
    assert is_it_friday() == False
```

9. Not Keeping Tests Up to Date

As your code evolves, your tests need to evolve with it. Outdated tests can give a false sense of security or become a maintenance burden.

Make updating tests part of your development process. When you change functionality, change the relevant tests at the same time.

10. Treating Test Code as Second-Class Code

It's easy to be less careful with test code than with production code, but remember that you'll need to maintain your tests too. Apply the same coding standards and practices to your test code as you do to your production code.

Advanced Unit Testing Techniques

Now that we've covered the basics and some common pitfalls, let's explore some advanced techniques that can take your unit testing to the next level.

Property-Based Testing

Property-based testing is a technique where instead of specifying exact inputs and outputs, you define properties that should always hold true for your function, and the testing framework generates random inputs to test these properties.

For example, let's say we have a function that reverses a list. Instead of writing individual test cases, we could define properties like:

1. The length of the reversed list should be the same as the original.
2. Reversing a reversed list should give the original list.
3. The first element of the reversed list should be the last element of the original list.

Here's how we might implement this using the hypothesis library in Python:

```
from hypothesis import given
import hypothesis.strategies as st


def reverse_list(lst):
    return lst[::-1]
```

```
@given(st.lists(st.integers()))
def test_reverse_list_properties(lst):
    reversed_lst = reverse_list(lst)

    # Property 1: Length should be the same
    assert len(reversed_lst) == len(lst)

    # Property 2: Reversing twice should give original list
    assert reverse_list(reversed_lst) == lst

    # Property 3: First element of reversed should be last of original
    if lst:
        assert reversed_lst[0] == lst[-1]
```

This test will run multiple times with different randomly generated lists, providing much more thorough testing than we could achieve with a few hand-written test cases.

Mutation Testing

Mutation testing is a way to test your tests. It works by making small changes (mutations) to your code and then running your tests. If your tests still pass after a mutation, it might indicate a weakness in your test suite.

For example, if you have a function:

```
def add(a, b):
    return a + b
```

A mutation testing tool might change it to:

```
def add(a, b):
    return a - b
```

If your tests still pass after this mutation, it suggests that your tests aren't thorough enough.

There are several mutation testing tools available for different languages. In Python, you might use a tool like mutmut:

```
mutmut run --paths-to-mutate=your_module.py
```

This will run your tests against various mutations of your code and report on which mutations were "killed" (caught by tests) and which "survived" (weren't caught).

Fuzzing

Fuzzing is a technique where you provide invalid, unexpected, or random data as inputs to your software. It's particularly useful for finding security vulnerabilities and edge cases that you might not have thought to test.

While traditionally used more in security testing, fuzzing can also be applied to unit testing. Many property-based testing frameworks, like hypothesis in Python, incorporate elements of fuzzing.

Here's a simple example of using hypothesis for fuzz testing:

```
from hypothesis import given, strategies as st


def parse_date(date_string):
    # Assume this function parses dates in the format "YYYY-MM-DD"
    year, month, day = map(int, date_string.split('-'))
    return datetime(year, month, day)


@given(st.text())
def test_parse_date_fuzzing(s):
    try:
        parse_date(s)
    except ValueError:
        # It's okay if it raises a ValueError for invalid inputs
```

```
    pass
  # If it doesn't raise a ValueError, it should return a valid date
  else:
    assert isinstance(parse_date(s), datetime)
```

This test will throw all kinds of random strings at our parse_date function, helping us find edge cases we might have missed.

Parameterized Tests

We touched on this earlier, but it's worth exploring in more depth. Parameterized tests allow you to run the same test multiple times with different inputs. This is particularly useful when you want to test a function with many different inputs without writing a separate test for each.

Here's an example using pytest:

```
import pytest


def is_prime(n):
  if n < 2:
    return False
  for i in range(2, int(n ** 0.5) + 1):
    if n % i == 0:
      return False
  return True


@pytest.mark.parametrize("number,expected", [
  (2, True),
  (3, True),
  (4, False),
  (5, True),
```

```
    (6, False),
    (7, True),
    (8, False),
    (9, False),
    (97, True),
])
def test_is_prime(number, expected):
    assert is_prime(number) == expected
```

This single test function will be run 9 times, once for each set of parameters. This makes it easy to test many different inputs without repeating code.

Behavior-Driven Development (BDD)

Behavior-Driven Development is an extension of Test-Driven Development that emphasizes collaboration between developers, QA, and non-technical stakeholders. It involves writing tests in a natural language style that non-programmers can understand.

In Python, you might use a library like behave for this:

```
Feature: User registration

  Scenario: Successful registration
    Given a user is not registered
    When they register with valid details
    Then their account should be created
    And they should receive a welcome email
```

This can then be implemented in Python:

```
from behave import *


@given('a user is not registered')
```

```
def step_impl(context):

    context.user = {'email': 'newuser@example.com', 'password': 'validpassword'}


@when('they register with valid details')

def step_impl(context):

    context.result = register_user(context.user['email'], context.user['password'])


@then('their account should be created')

def step_impl(context):

    assert context.result['success'] == True

    assert get_user(context.user['email']) is not None


@then('they should receive a welcome email')

def step_impl(context):

    assert check_email_sent(context.user['email'], 'Welcome')
```

This style of testing can be particularly useful for testing user stories and ensuring that your code meets business requirements.

Continuous Integration and Unit Testing

Unit tests are most effective when they're run frequently, ideally every time code changes. This is where Continuous Integration (CI) comes in.

CI is the practice of automatically building and testing your code every time you push changes to your version control system. Many CI tools, like Jenkins, Travis CI, CircleCI, and GitHub Actions, have built-in support for running unit tests.

Here's an example of a simple GitHub Actions workflow that runs Python tests:

```
name: Python tests


on: [push]
```

```
jobs:
  build:
    runs-on: ubuntu-latest
    steps:
    - uses: actions/checkout@v2
    - name: Set up Python
      uses: actions/setup-python@v2
      with:
        python-version: '3.x'
    - name: Install dependencies
      run: |
        python -m pip install --upgrade pip
        pip install -r requirements.txt
    - name: Run tests
      run: |
        python -m pytest
```

This workflow will run your tests every time you push to your GitHub repository, giving you immediate feedback if something breaks.

Conclusion

Unit testing is a powerful tool in a developer's arsenal. It helps catch bugs early, improves code quality, and gives you confidence in your code. But like any tool, it needs to be used correctly to be effective.

Remember:

1. Write tests early, ideally before or while writing your code.
2. Keep your tests focused and maintainable.
3. Use a variety of testing techniques, from simple assertions to property-based testing.

4. Don't just test the happy path - consider edge cases and error conditions.
5. Keep your tests fast and run them often, ideally as part of a CI pipeline.

As you continue to develop your unit testing skills, you'll find that it becomes an integral part of your development process, leading to more robust, reliable code. Happy testing!

Chapter 10: Integration Testing Approaches

Introduction: The Critical Role of Integration Testing

Welcome to the world of integration testing! If you've been following along with our journey through the Software Development Life Cycle (SDLC), you're probably feeling pretty good about your unit tests by now. But here's the thing: while unit tests are great for ensuring individual components work as expected, they don't tell us much about how these components play together in the grand symphony of our software.

That's where integration testing comes in. It's like being the conductor of an orchestra – you need to make sure all the instruments (or in our case, software components) are not just playing their parts correctly, but also harmonizing beautifully together.

In this chapter, we'll explore the art and science of integration testing. We'll dive into continuous integration practices, learn how to set up and manage test environments, and discover the power of automated integration testing tools. So, grab your baton (or your keyboard), and let's start conducting!

Continuous Integration: The Backbone of Modern Integration Testing

What is Continuous Integration?

Imagine you're building a massive jigsaw puzzle with a team. Now, wouldn't it be a nightmare if everyone worked on their pieces in isolation for weeks, only to find out at the end that they don't fit together? That's exactly the problem continuous integration (CI) solves in software development.

Continuous Integration is a development practice where team members integrate their work frequently, usually multiple times a day. Each integration is verified by an automated build and automated tests. By integrating regularly, you can detect errors quickly and locate them more easily.

The CI Process: A Day in the Life

Let me walk you through a typical day with CI:

1. You write some code and commit it to your version control system.
2. The CI server detects the change and starts a new build.
3. The code is compiled (if necessary) and unit tests are run.
4. If everything passes, integration tests are executed.
5. You receive feedback on the success or failure of the build.

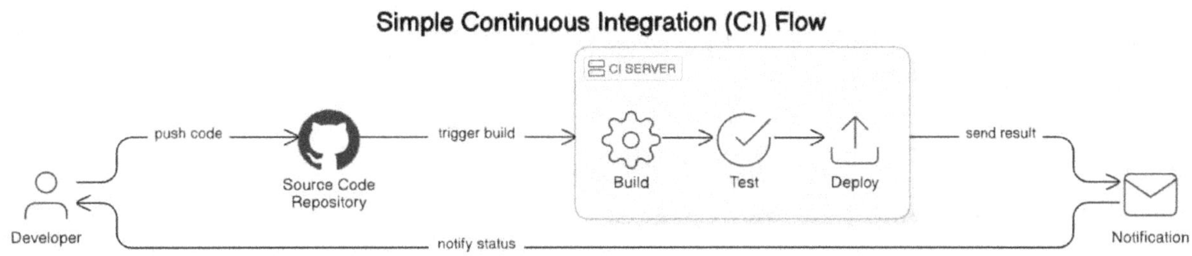

This process happens multiple times a day, for every developer on the team. It's like having a vigilant guardian constantly checking the health of your codebase.

Benefits of CI in Integration Testing

CI brings several benefits to the table:

1. **Early Bug Detection**: By integrating frequently, you catch integration issues early when they're easier and cheaper to fix.
2. **Reduced Integration Risk**: Remember the jigsaw puzzle analogy? CI ensures pieces fit together as you go, reducing the risk of a big integration headache at the end.
3. **Increased Visibility**: The whole team can see the state of the system at any time, fostering better collaboration.
4. **Faster Release Cycles**: With integration happening continuously, you're always close to a releasable state.

CI Best Practices

To make the most of CI, consider these best practices:

1. **Maintain a Single Source Repository**: All code and scripts needed to build the project should be in one place.
2. **Automate the Build**: You should be able to build and launch your system with a single command.

3. **Make the Build Self-Testing**: Include automated tests in the build process.
4. **Keep the Build Fast**: Aim for a build that takes no more than 10 minutes.
5. **Test in a Clone of the Production Environment**: Your test environment should mirror production as closely as possible.
6. **Make It Easy to Get the Latest Deliverables**: Anyone should be able to get the latest executable and release notes easily.
7. **Everyone Can See What's Happening**: Make the state of the build visible to everyone on the team.

Setting Up and Managing Test Environments

The Importance of a Good Test Environment

Have you ever tried on clothes in a dimly lit changing room, only to find they look completely different in daylight? That's what it's like testing software in an environment that doesn't match production. Your test environment is crucial – it's where your integration tests will live and breathe.

Types of Test Environments

In an ideal world, you'd have several types of environments:

1. **Development Environment**: Where developers write and test their code.
2. **Integration Environment**: Where code from multiple developers is combined and tested.
3. **Staging Environment**: A near-exact replica of production, used for final testing.
4. **Production Environment**: The live environment where real users interact with your software.

Each of these plays a role in ensuring your software is thoroughly tested before it reaches end-users.

Setting Up Your Test Environment

Here's a step-by-step guide to setting up a robust test environment:

1. **Define Your Requirements**: What do you need to test? What hardware and software will you need?

2. **Choose Your Infrastructure**: Will you use physical servers, virtual machines, or cloud services?
3. **Install Necessary Software**: This includes your application, databases, web servers, and any other required components.
4. **Configure the Environment**: Set up networking, security settings, and any necessary integrations.
5. **Load Test Data**: Populate your environment with realistic test data.
6. **Set Up Monitoring and Logging**: Ensure you can track what's happening in your environment.
7. **Document Everything**: Create clear documentation on how to use and maintain the environment.

Managing Test Environments

Managing test environments can be as challenging as setting them up. Here are some tips:

1. **Use Configuration Management Tools**: Tools like Ansible, Puppet, or Chef can help you maintain consistent environments.
2. **Implement Version Control**: Keep track of changes to your environment configurations.
3. **Automate Environment Creation**: Use scripts or tools to spin up new environments quickly.
4. **Regular Maintenance**: Keep your environments up-to-date with the latest patches and updates.
5. **Monitor Usage**: Keep an eye on who's using the environments and for what purpose.
6. **Clean Up Regularly**: Delete or archive old test data and unused environments to save resources.

Automated Integration Testing Tools

The Power of Automation in Integration Testing

Remember when we talked about CI and how it runs tests automatically? Well, those tests don't write themselves (at least not yet – who knows what AI will be capable of in a few years!). This is where automated integration testing tools come in.

These tools allow you to write tests that simulate real user interactions with your system, checking how different components work together. They can run these tests automatically, providing quick feedback on whether your latest changes have broken anything.

Popular Automated Integration Testing Tools

Let's look at some of the stars of the automated testing world:

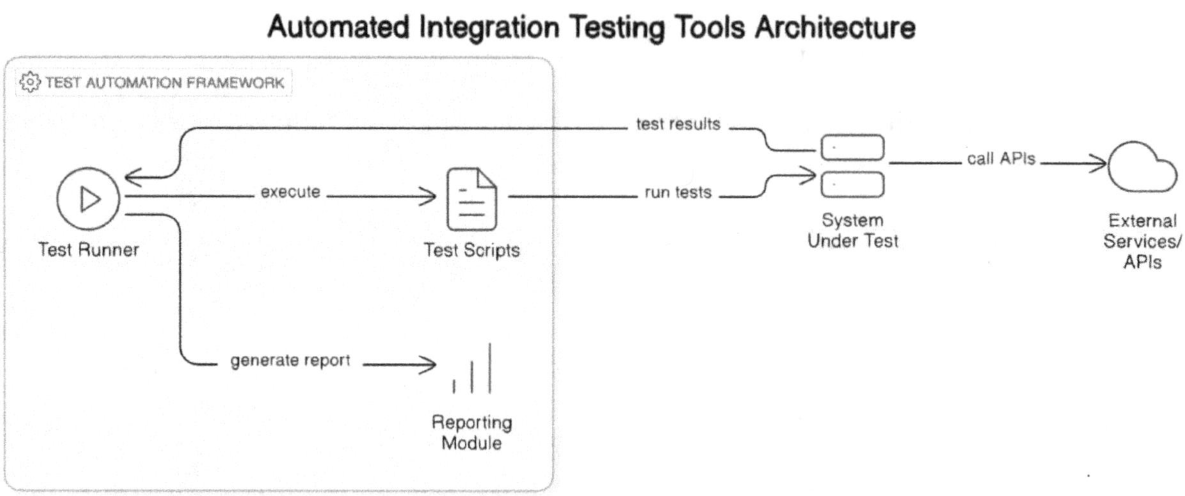

Selenium: The go-to tool for web application testing. It can automate browsers, simulating user interactions with your web app.

```
from selenium import webdriver

driver = webdriver.Chrome()
driver.get("https://www.example.com")
element = driver.find_element_by_id("login-button")
element.click()
```

1. **JUnit**: A simple framework to write repeatable tests for Java applications.

```
@Test
public void testAddition() {
  Calculator calc = new Calculator();
  assertEquals(4, calc.add(2, 2));
}
```

2. **TestNG**: Another testing framework for Java, with more advanced features than JUnit.

```
@Test(groups = {"integration"})
public void testDatabaseConnection() {
  Database db = new Database();
  assertTrue(db.connect());
}
```

3. **Jenkins**: Not strictly a testing tool, but a popular CI server that can run your tests automatically.

4. **Postman**: Great for testing APIs. You can write tests for your API responses and automate them.

```
pm.test("Status code is 200", function () {
  pm.response.to.have.status(200);
});
```

5. **Docker**: While primarily a containerization platform, Docker is incredibly useful for creating consistent test environments.

```
FROM python:3.8
COPY . /app
WORKDIR /app
RUN pip install -r requirements.txt
CMD ["python", "run_tests.py"]
```

Writing Effective Automated Integration Tests

Here are some tips for writing integration tests that will serve you well:

1. **Focus on Integration Points**: Test the interactions between components, not the components themselves (that's what unit tests are for).

2. **Use Realistic Data**: Your tests should use data that's as close to production data as possible.

3. **Test Happy Paths and Edge Cases**: Don't just test that things work when everything goes right. Test failure scenarios too.

4. **Keep Tests Independent**: Each test should be able to run on its own, without depending on the state left by other tests.

5. **Use Descriptive Test Names**: A good test name tells you what's being tested and under what conditions.

6. **Don't Overdo It**: You can't test everything. Focus on the most critical paths through your system.

Implementing a CI/CD Pipeline with Integration Tests

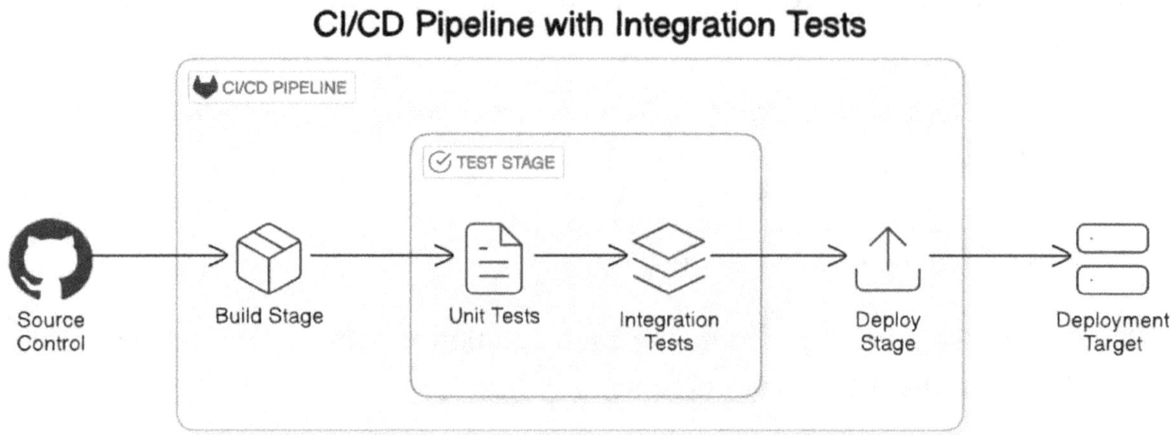

Now that we've covered the individual pieces, let's put it all together into a CI/CD pipeline that incorporates integration testing.

Step 1: Code Commit

It all starts when a developer commits code to the version control system. This triggers the CI/CD pipeline.

Step 2: Build

The code is compiled (if necessary) and packaged into a deployable unit.

Step 3: Unit Tests

The first line of defense! Unit tests are run to catch any obvious issues.

Step 4: Deploy to Test Environment

If unit tests pass, the code is deployed to a test environment that mirrors production.

Step 5: Integration Tests

Now it's time for the star of our show – integration tests are run in the test environment.

```
def test_user_registration_and_login():
    # Register a new user
    user = register_new_user("testuser", "password123")
    assert user is not None
```

```
# Try to log in with the new user
logged_in_user = login_user("testuser", "password123")
assert logged_in_user == user

# Check if user can access a protected resource
response = access_protected_resource(logged_in_user)
assert response.status_code == 200
```

Step 6: Additional Tests

If integration tests pass, you might run additional tests like performance tests or security scans.

Step 7: Manual Testing/UAT

For critical changes, you might include a manual testing or user acceptance testing (UAT) step.

Step 8: Deploy to Production

If all tests pass and approvals are received, the code is deployed to production.

Step 9: Monitoring

After deployment, monitor the application closely for any issues that might have slipped through testing.

Challenges in Integration Testing

While integration testing is crucial, it's not without its challenges. Let's look at some common hurdles and how to overcome them:

1. Test Environment Management

Challenge: Maintaining test environments that accurately reflect production can be difficult and resource-intensive.

Solution: Use containerization technologies like Docker to create consistent, reproducible environments. Infrastructure-as-Code tools like Terraform can also help manage complex environments.

2. Test Data Management

Challenge: Creating and maintaining realistic test data can be time-consuming and complex.

Solution: Invest in good test data generation tools. Consider using anonymized production data (ensuring you comply with data protection regulations).

3. Dealing with External Dependencies

Challenge: Integration tests often involve systems you don't control, like third-party APIs.

Solution: Use mocking frameworks to simulate external dependencies. For critical integrations, consider setting up a test instance of the external system.

4. Slow Feedback Loop

Challenge: Integration tests can be slow, especially as your system grows.

Solution: Optimize your tests and your CI pipeline. Run tests in parallel where possible. Consider implementing a test pyramid, with more unit tests and fewer integration tests.

5. Flaky Tests

Challenge: Integration tests can be inconsistent, passing sometimes and failing others without code changes.

Solution: Identify and fix sources of non-determinism in your tests. This might involve adding retries for network operations or ensuring test isolation.

Best Practices for Integration Testing

To wrap up, let's review some best practices that will help you get the most out of your integration testing efforts:

1. **Start Early**: Don't wait until the end of development to start integration testing. The earlier you start, the earlier you'll catch issues.
2. **Automate as Much as Possible**: Manual integration testing is time-consuming and error-prone. Automate your tests to run them frequently and consistently.
3. **Use Continuous Integration**: As we discussed earlier, CI is a powerful tool for catching integration issues early.
4. **Test in Production-Like Environments**: The closer your test environment is to production, the more confidence you can have in your tests.

5. **Monitor Test Coverage**: While 100% coverage isn't necessary (or even desirable) for integration tests, you should keep an eye on your coverage to ensure you're testing the most important paths through your system.
6. **Keep Tests Independent**: Each test should set up its own data and clean up after itself. This prevents tests from interfering with each other.
7. **Use Descriptive Test Names**: A good test name describes the scenario being tested and the expected outcome.
8. **Review and Maintain Your Tests**: Your integration tests are part of your codebase. Review them regularly and keep them up-to-date as your system evolves.
9. **Balance Speed and Comprehensiveness**: While thorough testing is important, if your integration tests take hours to run, they'll be run less frequently. Strike a balance between coverage and speed.
10. **Learn from Failures**: When an integration test fails, it's an opportunity to learn. Analyze failures to understand not just what went wrong, but why.

Conclusion: Embracing the Integration Testing Mindset

As we wrap up our exploration of integration testing, I hope you're feeling excited about the possibilities. Integration testing is more than just a phase in the SDLC – it's a mindset, a way of thinking about your system as a whole rather than as isolated components.

By embracing continuous integration, setting up robust test environments, leveraging automated testing tools, and following best practices, you're not just catching bugs – you're building confidence. Confidence that your system works as a cohesive whole. Confidence that you can make changes without breaking existing functionality. Confidence that you're delivering value to your users.

Remember, integration testing is a journey, not a destination. As your system evolves, so too should your integration testing strategy. Stay curious, keep learning, and never stop asking, "How can we test this better?"

In our next chapter, we'll build on what we've learned here as we dive into system testing methodologies. We'll explore how to test your entire system from end to end, ensuring it meets both functional and non-functional requirements. So, keep your testing hat on – the adventure continues!

Chapter 11: System Testing Methodologies

Introduction

Welcome to the world of system testing! If you've made it this far in your software development journey, you're probably feeling a mix of excitement and trepidation. On one hand, you're closer than ever to releasing your software into the wild. On the other hand, you're faced with the daunting task of ensuring that your creation works as intended, can handle real-world scenarios, and won't crumble under pressure. Don't worry, I've been there too, and I'm here to guide you through the intricate maze of system testing methodologies.

In this chapter, we'll explore the various approaches to system testing that will help you build confidence in your software's readiness for prime time. We'll dive into functional and non-functional testing, performance and load testing, and even tackle the ever-important realm of security testing. By the end of this chapter, you'll have a comprehensive toolkit to put your software through its paces and catch those sneaky bugs before they have a chance to embarrass you in front of your users.

Functional Testing: Ensuring Your Software Does What It's Supposed To

Let's start with the basics – functional testing. This is where we make sure that your software does what it says on the tin. Remember that list of requirements you painstakingly gathered way back in Chapter 2? Well, now's the time to put them to the test!

Test Case Design

The first step in functional testing is designing your test cases. Think of these as a series of experiments you'll conduct on your software. Each test case should:

1. Have a clear objective
2. Outline the steps to be taken
3. Specify the expected results

When I was working on a project for a large e-commerce platform, we had thousands of test cases. One of my favorites was the "Fat Finger Test" – we'd intentionally mistype product names to see if the search function could still find what we were looking for. It's amazing how many issues you can uncover by thinking like a clumsy user!

Black Box Testing

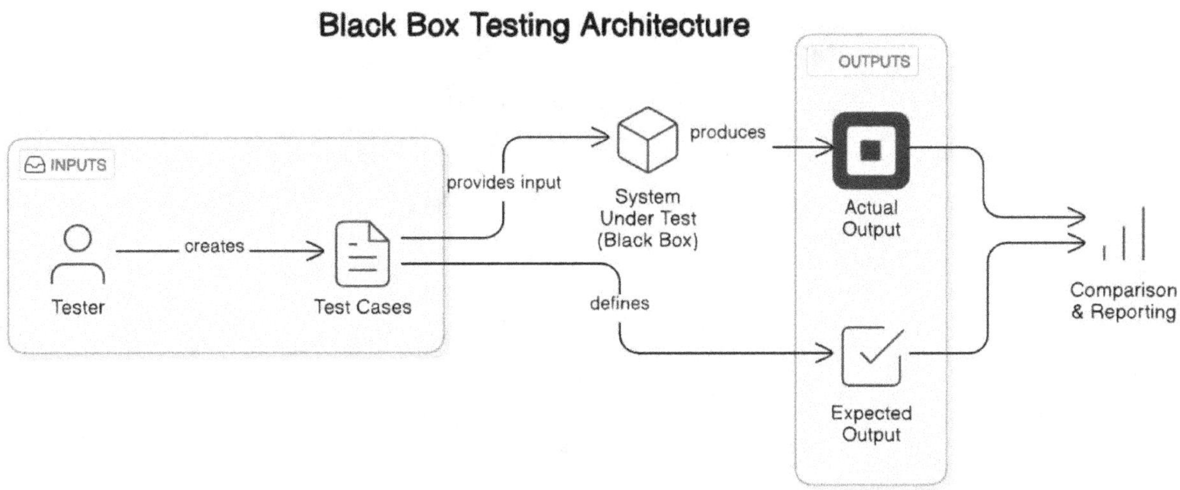

Black box testing is a method where the tester doesn't need to know the internal workings of the system. You're essentially treating the software as a black box – you provide inputs and check if the outputs match your expectations.

This approach is great for simulating real-world usage. After all, your users won't know (or care) about the intricate details of your code. They just want to click a button and have something happen!

White Box Testing

On the flip side, white box testing involves examining the internal structure of the software. This is where your development team gets to flex their muscles and ensure that the code is doing what it's supposed to do under the hood.

I once worked on a project where white box testing revealed that a critical calculation was using the wrong variable. It worked fine for most inputs, but would have caused major issues for edge cases. Catching that early saved us from a potential disaster down the line.

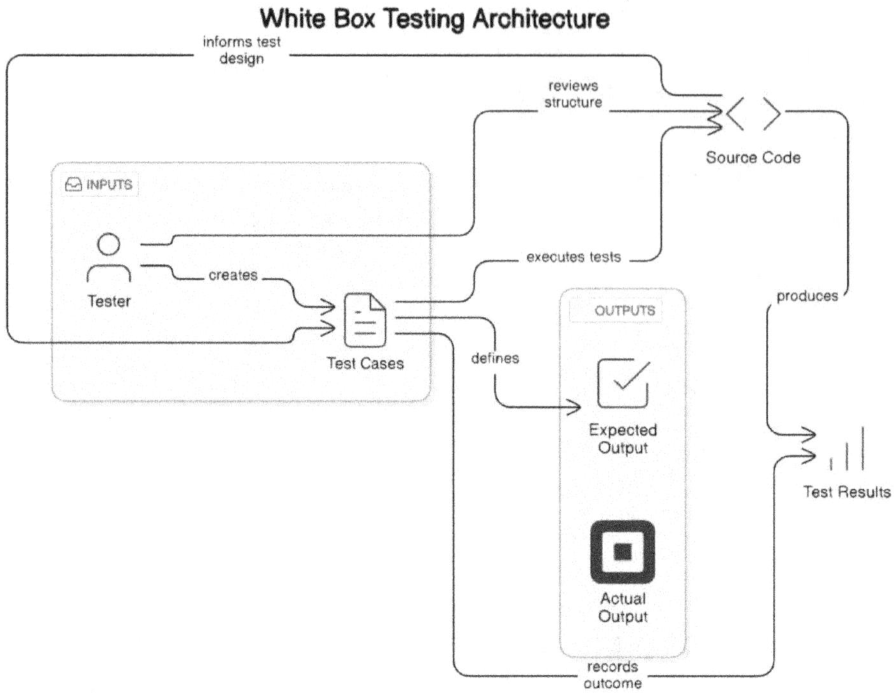

Regression Testing

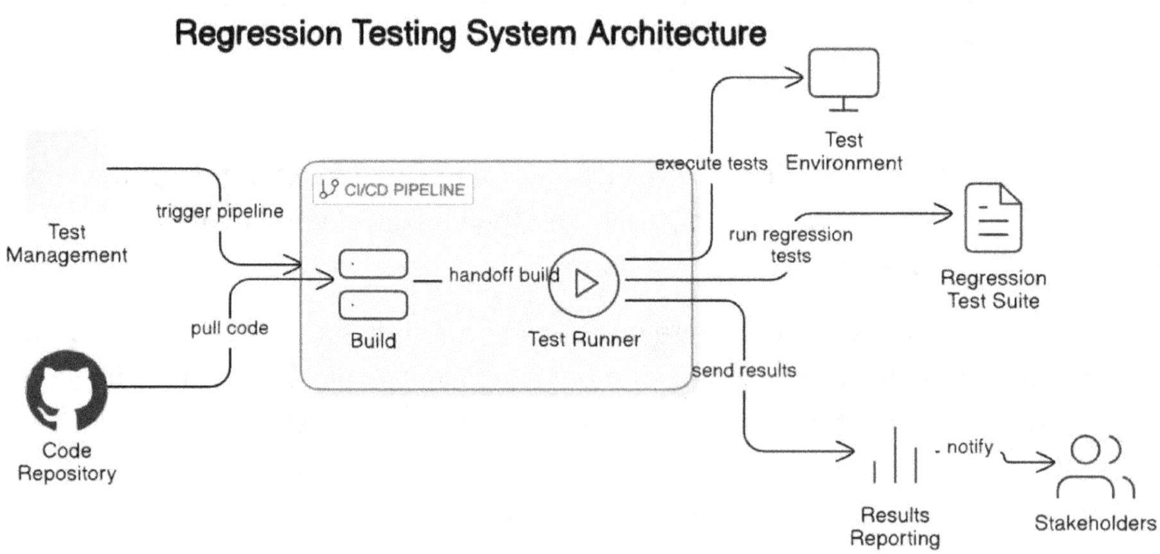

As you make changes and fix bugs, it's crucial to ensure that you haven't inadvertently broken something else. This is where regression testing comes in. You'll re-run previously completed tests to verify that existing functionalities still work as expected.

Pro tip: Automate your regression tests as much as possible. Trust me, you don't want to be manually clicking through hundreds of test cases every time you make a small change!

Non-Functional Testing: Because It's Not Just About Features

While functional testing ensures your software does what it's supposed to do, non-functional testing focuses on how well it does it. This is where we separate the good software from the great software.

Usability Testing

Usability testing is all about putting yourself in your users' shoes. Is your software intuitive? Can users accomplish their goals without pulling their hair out in frustration?

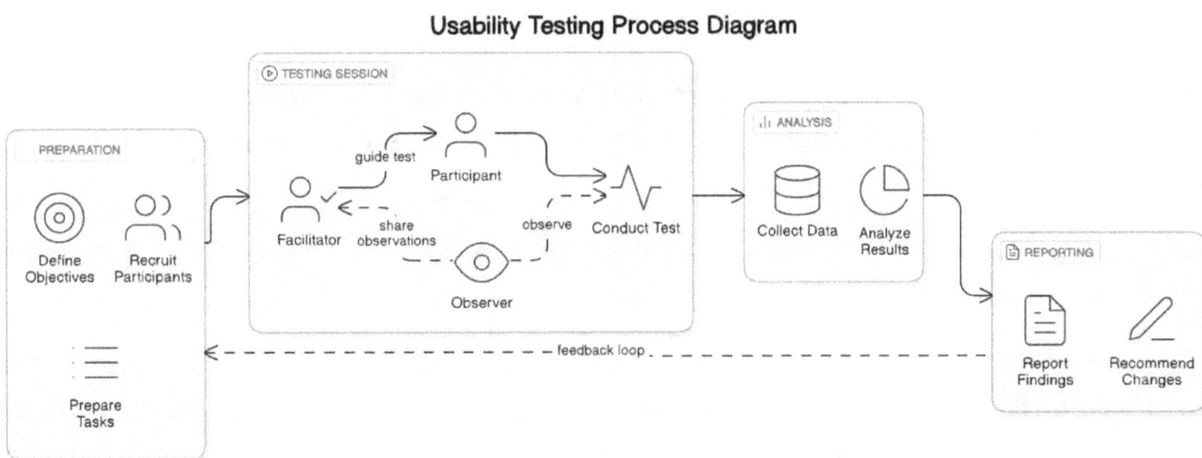

Sometimes, we thought we had designed the perfect user interface. But when we brought in some test users, they were completely lost. It taught us the importance of testing with real people, not just other developers.

Some key aspects to consider in usability testing:

1. Navigation: Can users easily find what they're looking for?
2. Clarity: Are instructions and labels clear and unambiguous?
3. Efficiency: Can tasks be completed with minimal steps?
4. Error handling: Are error messages helpful and actionable?

Accessibility Testing

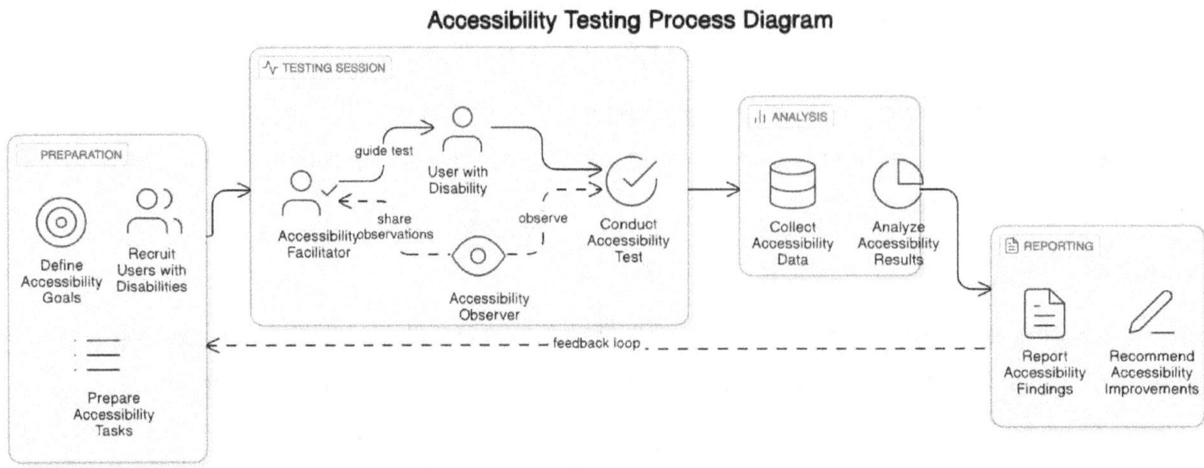

In today's world, it's crucial to ensure that your software is accessible to users with disabilities. This isn't just the right thing to do – in many cases, it's a legal requirement.

Accessibility testing involves checking that your software works well with assistive technologies like screen readers, and follows accessibility guidelines such as the Web Content Accessibility Guidelines (WCAG).

A personal anecdote: I once worked on a project where we implemented a beautiful drag-and-drop interface. It looked great and worked smoothly – for users who could use a mouse. We had completely forgotten about keyboard accessibility! Always remember to test your software with different input methods.

Compatibility Testing

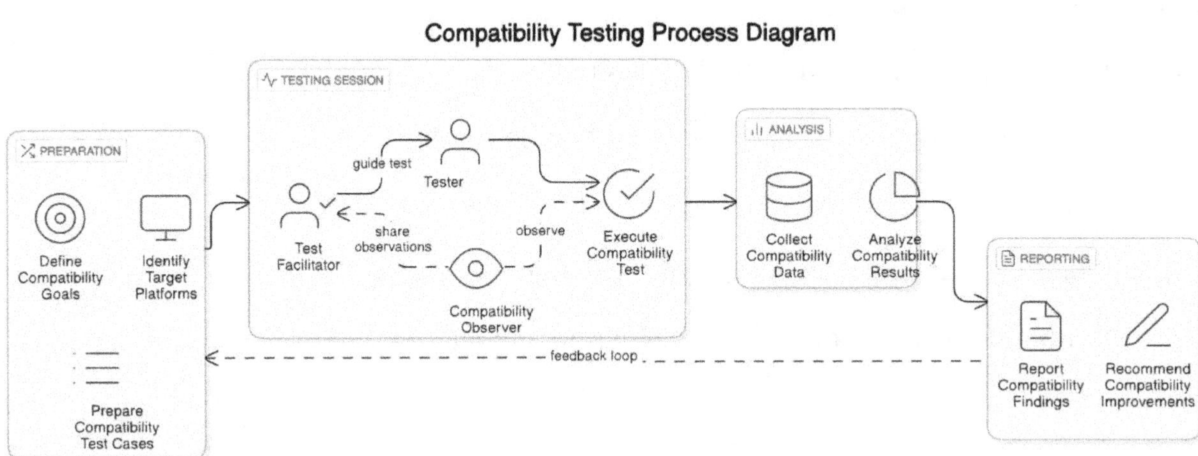

Unless you're developing for a very specific environment, your software will likely need to work across different platforms, browsers, or devices. Compatibility testing ensures that your software plays nice with various configurations.

This can be a Herculean task, especially for web applications. I remember a project where we had to support Internet Explorer 6 (yes, I'm that old). The number of hacks and workarounds we had to implement still gives me nightmares. Thankfully, modern browsers are much more standards-compliant, but it's still important to test across different environments.

Performance and Load Testing: Preparing for Success (and Stress)

Now that we know our software works correctly and is user-friendly, it's time to see how it performs under pressure. Performance and load testing are crucial for ensuring that your software can handle real-world usage without breaking a sweat.

Performance Testing

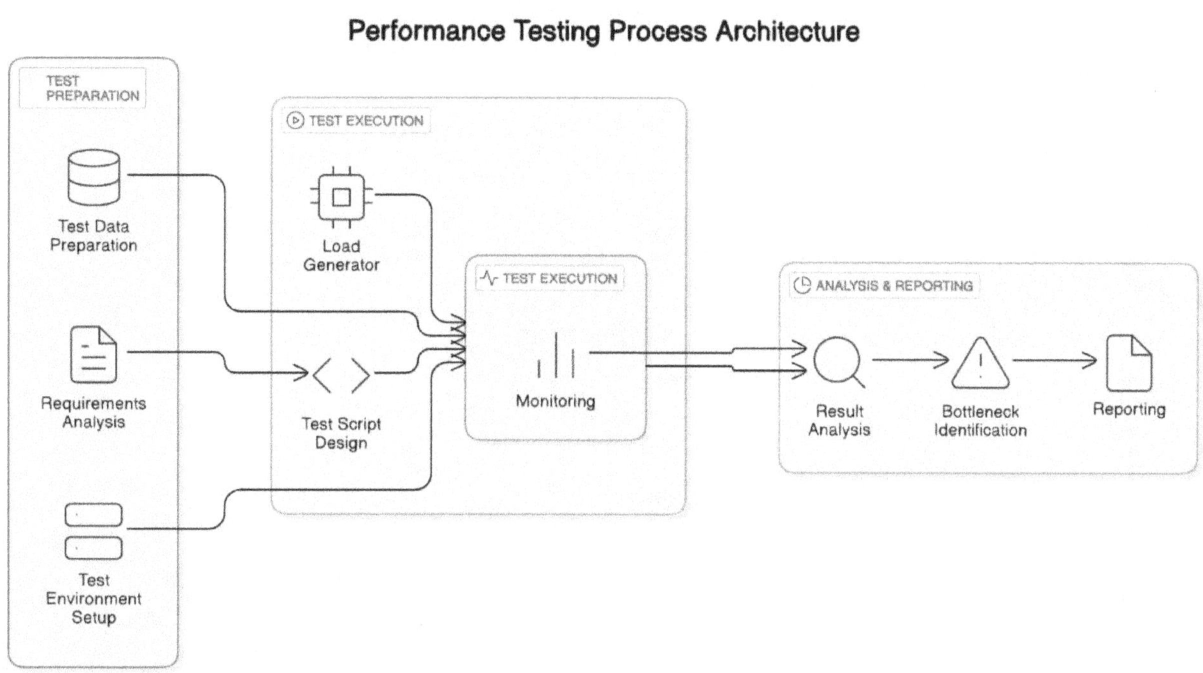

Performance testing is all about speed, responsiveness, and stability. You're looking at metrics like response time, throughput, and resource utilization.

High-performance applications like trading platforms demand microsecond-level optimizations, but even typical software must prioritize responsiveness to ensure a smooth user experience.

Key areas to focus on in performance testing:

1. Response time: How quickly does your software respond to user actions?
2. Throughput: How many transactions can your system handle per unit of time?
3. Resource utilization: How efficiently does your software use CPU, memory, and network resources?

Load Testing

Load testing takes performance testing a step further by simulating multiple users or high transaction volumes. The goal is to identify how your system behaves under expected load conditions.

E-commerce sites must undergo realistic and extreme load testing to avoid crashes during peak traffic events like Black Friday. Performance testing under simulated high-demand conditions is crucial for ensuring system reliability!

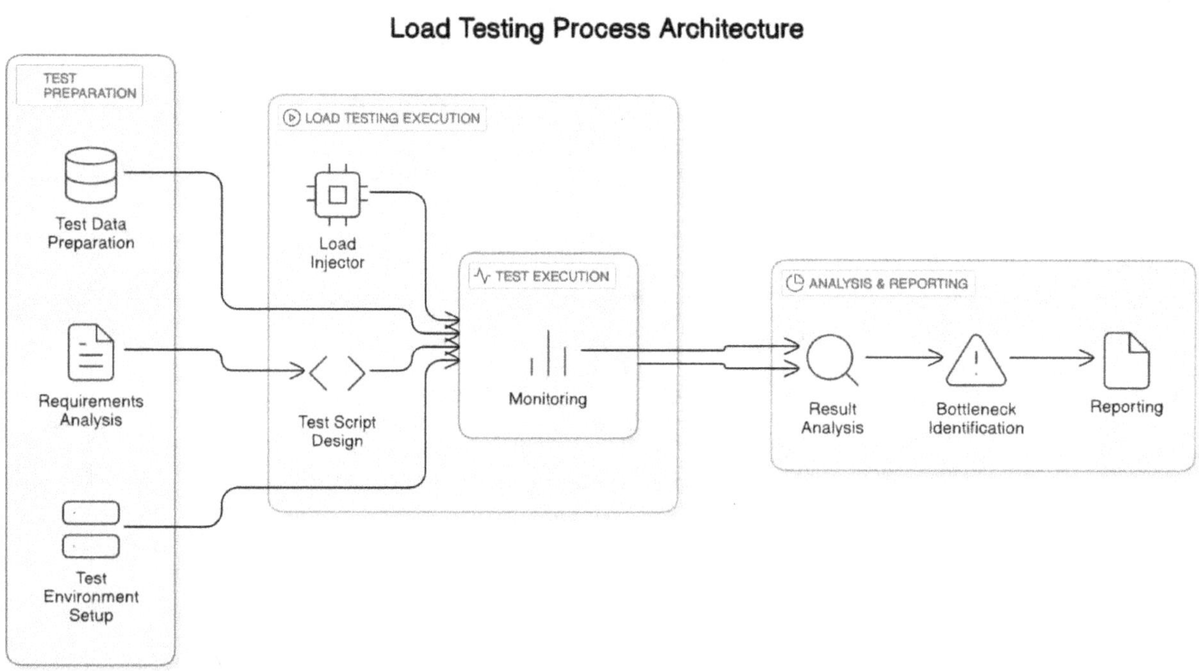

When conducting load tests, pay attention to:

1. Scalability: How does performance change as load increases?
2. Bottlenecks: Are there specific components that become overwhelmed under load?
3. Breaking point: At what point does the system start to degrade or fail?

Stress Testing

While load testing simulates expected conditions, stress testing pushes your system to its limits and beyond. The goal is to identify the breaking point and understand how the system fails.

In stress testing, you'll want to observe:

1. Failure behavior: Does the system fail gracefully or crash spectacularly?
2. Recovery: How quickly and effectively does the system recover after failure?
3. Error handling: Are errors properly logged and reported under extreme conditions?

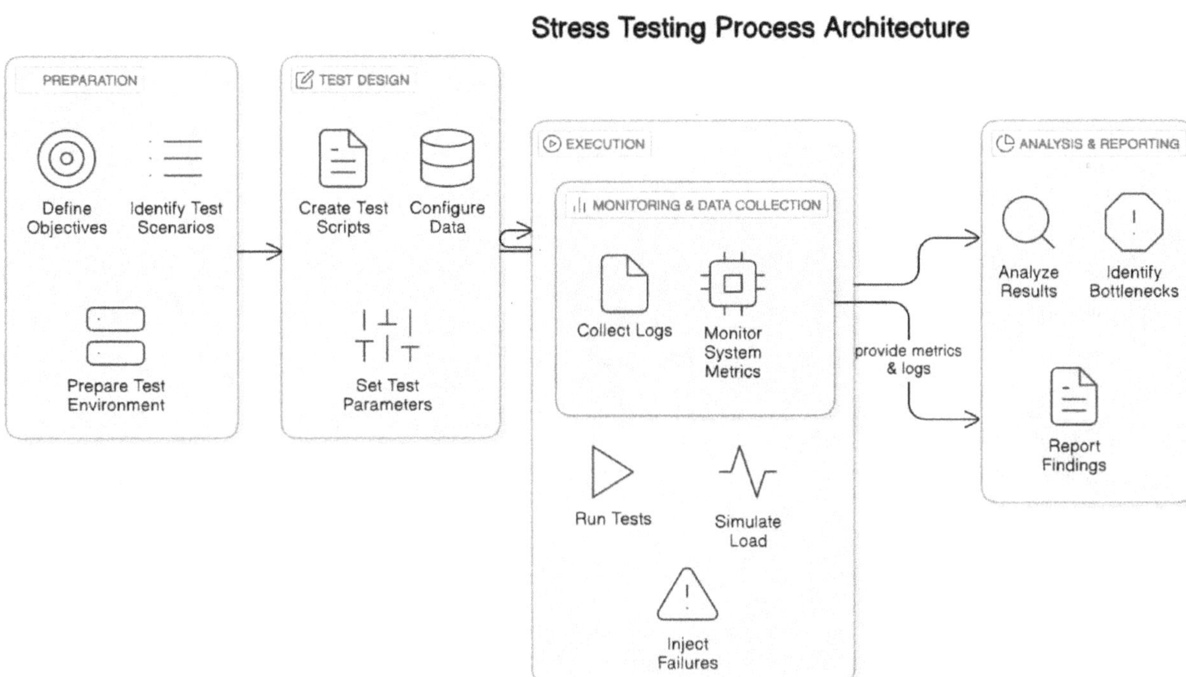

Endurance Testing

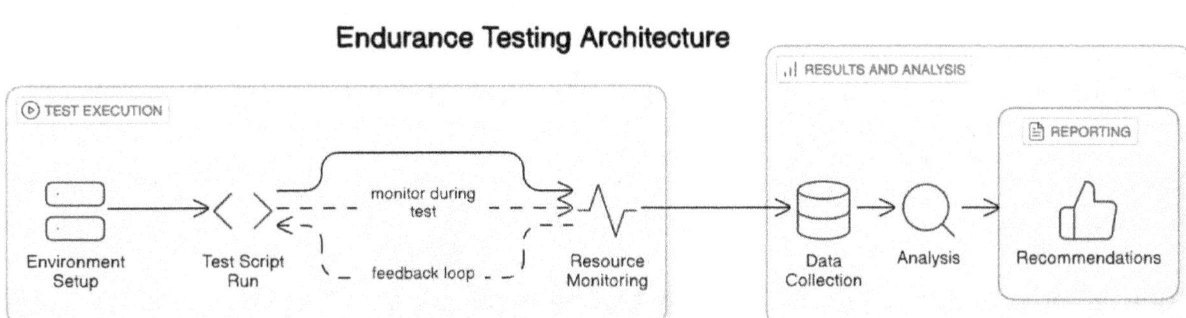

Also known as soak testing, endurance testing involves running your system under load for an extended period. This helps identify issues that might only appear after prolonged use, such as memory leaks or performance degradation.

I once worked on a system that performed flawlessly in short tests but would gradually slow down over time. It turned out we had a subtle memory leak that only became noticeable after several hours of operation. Endurance testing saved us from a lot of late-night emergency calls!

Security Testing: Protecting Your Software (and Your Users)

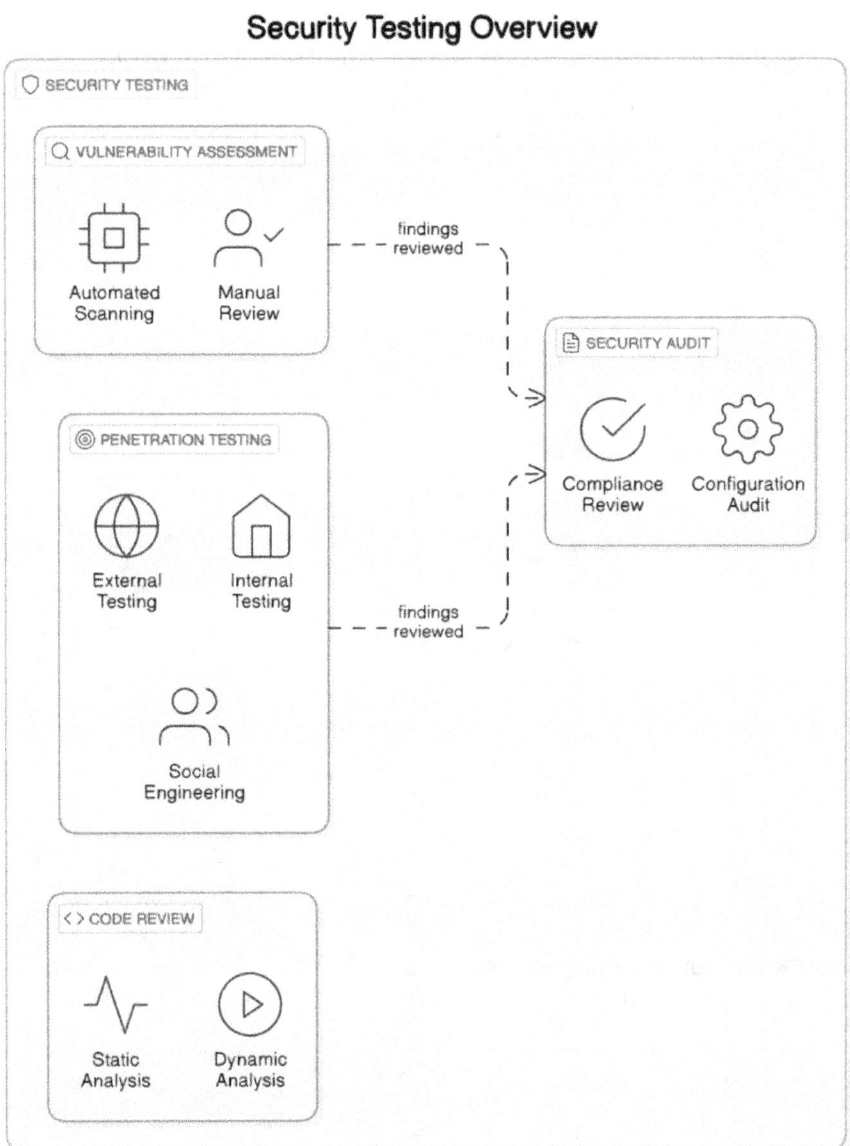

In today's interconnected world, security testing is more important than ever. It's not just about protecting your software – it's about safeguarding your users' data and maintaining their trust.

Vulnerability Scanning

Vulnerability scanning involves using automated tools to identify known security weaknesses in your software and its dependencies. These tools can help you catch common issues like outdated libraries with known vulnerabilities.

Pro tip: Integrate vulnerability scanning into your CI/CD pipeline. This way, you'll catch potential security issues early in the development process.

Penetration Testing

Penetration testing, or "pen testing," involves simulating attacks on your system to identify vulnerabilities. This is where you put on your "black hat" and try to break into your own system.

Penetration testing often reveals unexpected vulnerabilities—like information leaks through obscure error messages—demonstrating attackers' creativity. This underscores the necessity of adopting an adversarial mindset during security assessments to uncover and mitigate potential exploits.

Key areas to focus on in penetration testing:

1. Authentication and authorization: Can unauthorized users access restricted areas?
2. Input validation: Is the system vulnerable to injection attacks?
3. Session management: Can sessions be hijacked or manipulated?
4. Error handling: Do error messages reveal sensitive information?

Security Compliance Testing

Depending on your industry, you may need to comply with specific security standards or regulations. Security compliance testing ensures that your software meets these requirements.

Common standards include:

1. GDPR (General Data Protection Regulation)
2. HIPAA (Health Insurance Portability and Accountability Act)
3. PCI DSS (Payment Card Industry Data Security Standard)

Compliance testing can be complex and may require specialized knowledge. Don't hesitate to bring in experts if you're dealing with sensitive data or strict regulatory requirements.

Data Privacy Testing

With increasing concerns about data privacy, it's crucial to ensure that your software handles user data responsibly. Data privacy testing focuses on how data is collected, stored, used, and deleted.

Key aspects to consider:

1. Data collection: Is only necessary data being collected?
2. Data storage: Is sensitive data properly encrypted?
3. Data access: Are there proper controls on who can access user data?
4. Data deletion: Can users easily request deletion of their data?

Bringing It All Together: Creating a Comprehensive System Testing Strategy

Now that we've explored various system testing methodologies, it's time to bring it all together into a cohesive strategy. Remember, the goal is not to blindly apply every testing technique, but to create a tailored approach that fits your specific project and its requirements.

Prioritizing Test Types

Start by prioritizing the types of tests based on your project's needs. For a financial application, security and performance might be top priorities. For a social media app, usability and scalability might take precedence.

Creating a Test Plan

Develop a comprehensive test plan that outlines:

1. Test objectives
2. Testing methodologies to be used
3. Test environment specifications
4. Roles and responsibilities
5. Test schedule and milestones
6. Defect tracking and resolution process

Automating Where Possible

Automate as much of your testing as possible, especially for regression testing and performance testing. This will save time in the long run and allow for more frequent and consistent testing.

Continuous Testing

Integrate testing into your development process rather than treating it as a separate phase. Continuous testing helps catch issues earlier when they're easier and cheaper to fix.

Learning and Iterating

Finally, remember that system testing is an iterative process. Learn from each testing cycle and use those insights to improve both your software and your testing process.

Conclusion

Congratulations! You've now got a solid understanding of system testing methodologies. From functional testing to security testing, you're equipped with the knowledge to put your software through its paces and ensure it's ready for the real world.

Remember, thorough system testing is your best defense against embarrassing bugs, performance issues, and security vulnerabilities. It's not just about finding problems – it's about building confidence in your software and delivering a product that your users will love.

As you move forward in your software development journey, keep these testing methodologies in mind. They'll serve as your trusty tools for creating robust, performant, and secure software. And who knows? You might even start to enjoy the thrill of uncovering and squashing those elusive bugs!

In the next chapter, we'll dive into the world of User Acceptance Testing (UAT), where we'll see how all our hard work stands up to the ultimate test – real users. So take a deep breath, pat yourself on the back for mastering system testing, and get ready to face your toughest critics yet!

Chapter 12: User Acceptance Testing (UAT)

Introduction

Welcome to the exciting world of User Acceptance Testing (UAT)! If you've made it this far in your software development journey, you're on the brink of releasing your product to the world. But before you pop the champagne, there's one crucial step left: making sure your end-users are as thrilled about your software as you are.

Chapter 12: User Acceptance Testing (UAT)

In this chapter, we'll dive deep into the art and science of UAT. I'll guide you through the process of planning, preparing, and executing UAT to ensure your software not only meets technical requirements but also delights your users. So, buckle up, and let's explore how to make your software truly user-approved!

Understanding User Acceptance Testing

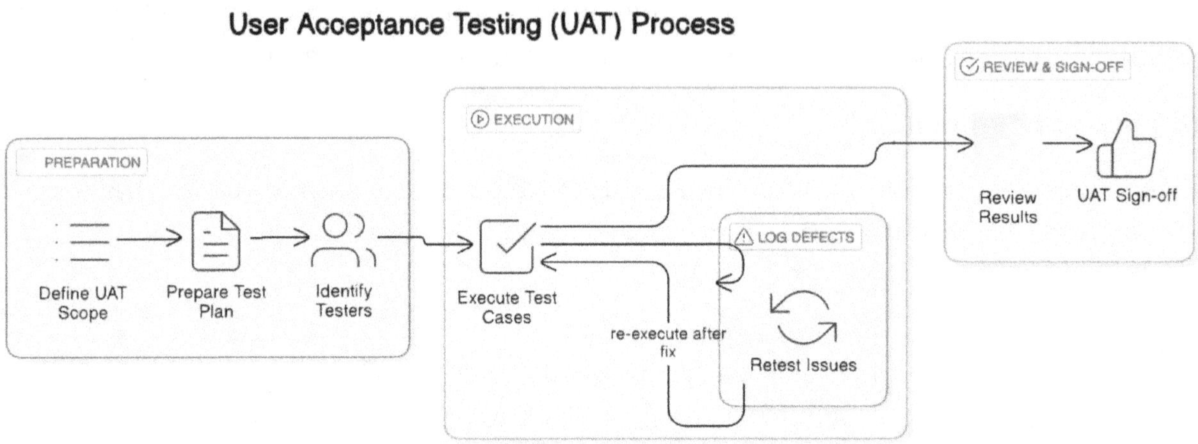

Before we roll up our sleeves and get into the nitty-gritty of UAT, let's take a moment to understand what it really means.

User Acceptance Testing is the final frontier in the testing phase of software development. It's where we hand over our precious creation to the people who matter most – the end-users. These are the folks who will be using your software day in and day out, and their stamp of approval is what we're after.

Even after extensive development and testing, user acceptance testing (UAT) often reveals overlooked usability issues that developers might miss. This highlights the critical importance of evaluating products from the end-user perspective to ensure they meet real-world needs.

UAT is not just another box to tick off in your project plan. It's your opportunity to validate that your software meets the business requirements and user needs in real-world scenarios. It's where you discover if your product is truly ready for prime time or if it needs a bit more polishing.

The Importance of UAT in the SDLC

You might be wondering, "Why do we need UAT when we've already done so much testing?" Well, let me tell you why it's crucial:

1. **Real-world validation**: While other testing phases focus on technical aspects, UAT simulates real-world usage. It's like a dress rehearsal before the big show.
2. **User perspective**: UAT brings in the perspective of actual users, which can be quite different from that of developers or testers.
3. **Business requirement verification**: It ensures that the software aligns with business goals and user needs.
4. **Usability assessment**: UAT helps identify usability issues that might have been overlooked in earlier stages.
5. **Change management**: It prepares users for the new system, easing the transition and adoption process.
6. **Confidence building**: Successful UAT builds confidence among stakeholders and users in the new system.

UAT Planning and Preparation

Now that we understand the importance of UAT, let's roll up our sleeves and get into the planning and preparation phase. Remember, failing to plan is planning to fail, especially when it comes to UAT.

Identifying Key Stakeholders

The first step in UAT planning is identifying who needs to be involved. This typically includes:

- End-users from different departments or user groups
- Business analysts who can verify business requirements
- Project managers to oversee the process
- Technical support staff to assist with any issues

Excluding key department representatives from UAT often leads to unmet requirements and costly rework. Thorough stakeholder identification ensures all critical perspectives are considered during user acceptance testing!

Defining UAT Objectives and Scope

Clear objectives and scope are crucial for successful UAT. Ask yourself:

- What are the critical functions that need to be tested?
- What are the acceptance criteria for each function?

- Are there any specific business scenarios that need to be validated?
- What is out of scope for this UAT?

Document these clearly and get sign-off from key stakeholders. This will be your north star throughout the UAT process.

Creating a UAT Plan

Your UAT plan is your roadmap. It should include:

1. **Timeline**: When will UAT start and end? Include buffer time for unexpected issues.
2. **Resources**: Who will participate? What roles will they play?
3. **Environment**: Where will UAT be conducted? Ensure it mirrors the production environment as closely as possible.
4. **Training**: How will you prepare users for UAT?
5. **Support**: Who will provide technical support during UAT?
6. **Feedback mechanism**: How will users report issues or provide feedback?

Preparing the UAT Environment

Setting up the right environment is crucial for effective UAT. Here's what you need to consider:

1. **Data**: Populate the system with realistic data. If possible, use anonymized production data.
2. **Infrastructure**: Ensure the hardware and network setup closely resembles the production environment.
3. **Access**: Set up user accounts and necessary permissions for all participants.
4. **Tools**: Prepare any necessary tools for testing and feedback collection.

Designing Test Cases for End-Users

Now that we've laid the groundwork, it's time to design test cases. But remember, these aren't your typical technical test cases. We're designing for end-users, so we need to think like them.

Understanding User Workflows

Start by mapping out the key workflows that users will follow in your software. For example, if you're testing an e-commerce platform, typical workflows might include:

1. Browsing products
2. Adding items to cart
3. Checking out
4. Tracking an order

For each workflow, break it down into steps that a user would follow. This forms the basis of your test cases.

Creating User-Friendly Test Cases

When writing test cases for UAT, keep these principles in mind:

1. **Use plain language**: Avoid technical jargon. Write as if you're explaining to a friend.
2. **Be specific**: Provide clear, step-by-step instructions.
3. **Include expected results**: Clearly state what the user should expect to see or happen.
4. **Cover edge cases**: Include scenarios that test the boundaries of the system.

Here's an example of a user-friendly test case:

```
Test Case: Place an Order

Steps:

1. Log in to your account

2. Search for "blue t-shirt"

3. Click on any blue t-shirt in the results

4. Select your size and click "Add to Cart"

5. Click on the shopping cart icon

6. Click "Proceed to Checkout"

7. Fill in shipping details and payment information
```

8. Click "Place Order"

Expected Result:

- You should see an order confirmation page

- You should receive an email with your order details

Prioritizing Test Cases

Not all test cases are created equal. Prioritize your test cases based on:

1. **Criticality**: How important is this function to the core business?
2. **Frequency of use**: How often will users perform this action?
3. **Risk**: What's the potential impact if this function fails?

A High/Medium/Low prioritization system helps maintain focus during UAT, especially when time constraints arise. This approach ensures critical issues are addressed first while efficiently managing testing efforts..

Conducting UAT Sessions

With our plan in place and test cases ready, it's time for the main event: conducting UAT sessions. This is where the rubber meets the road, and we get to see our software through our users' eyes.

Kick-off Meeting

Start with a kick-off meeting to:

1. Introduce the UAT team and their roles
2. Review the UAT objectives and timeline
3. Explain the process for executing test cases and reporting issues
4. Set expectations for communication and support during UAT

Guiding Users Through Test Cases

As users work through the test cases:

1. Be available to answer questions or clarify instructions
2. Encourage users to think aloud as they navigate the software

3. Observe their interactions closely – sometimes what they don't say is as important as what they do
4. Take notes on any difficulties or confusion they experience

Observing users interact with a system often reveals unexpected usability challenges, even for features presumed intuitive. Silent observation provides unbiased insights that drive meaningful interface improvements.

Capturing Feedback

Implement a systematic way to capture feedback:

1. **Issue tracking system**: Use a tool like Jira or Trello to log and track issues.
2. **Feedback forms**: Provide forms for users to document their experiences after each session.
3. **Debriefing sessions**: Hold short debriefs after each UAT session to gather immediate impressions.

Remember, not all feedback will be about bugs. Users might suggest improvements or identify missing features. Capture these ideas too – they're gold dust for future iterations!

Defect Tracking and Resolution

As issues start rolling in during UAT, you need a robust process to track and resolve them. Here's how to manage this crucial aspect of UAT:

Categorizing Defects

Not all defects are created equal. Categorize them to help prioritize fixes:

1. **Severity**: How much does this impact the user's ability to use the software?
    - Critical: System crash or data loss
    - High: Major function is broken
    - Medium: Function works but with significant problems
    - Low: Minor issue, easy workaround available
2. **Type**: What kind of issue is it?
    - Functional: Something doesn't work as specified
    - Usability: It works, but it's difficult or confusing to use

- Performance: It's too slow or resource-intensive
- Security: Potential vulnerability or data protection issue

Prioritizing Fixes

With limited time and resources, you need to prioritize which issues to fix. Consider:

1. Severity of the issue
2. Frequency of occurrence
3. Number of users affected
4. Effort required to fix

Use a simple 2x2 matrix of Impact vs Effort to visualize and decide on priorities.

Managing the Defect Lifecycle

Implement a clear process for managing defects:

1. **Reporting**: User reports an issue
2. **Triage**: Team reviews and categorizes the issue
3. **Assignment**: Issue is assigned to a developer
4. **Resolution**: Developer fixes the issue
5. **Verification**: Fix is verified by QA
6. **Closure**: Issue is closed after user confirmation

Communicate clearly with users about the status of their reported issues. Nothing frustrates a UAT participant more than feeling their feedback is going into a black hole!

Retesting and Regression Testing

As fixes are implemented:

1. Retest the specific issue to ensure it's resolved
2. Conduct regression testing to ensure the fix hasn't broken anything else

Consider involving the original user who reported the issue in retesting. Their confirmation can be a powerful stamp of approval.

Analyzing UAT Results

As UAT progresses, you'll accumulate a wealth of data and feedback. Analyzing this information is crucial to determine if your software is ready for release.

Quantitative Analysis

Look at the numbers:

1. **Test case pass/fail rates**: What percentage of test cases passed on the first attempt?
2. **Defect metrics**: How many defects were found? What's their severity distribution?
3. **User satisfaction scores**: If you've used satisfaction surveys, analyze the results.

These metrics give you a high-level view of your software's readiness.

Qualitative Analysis

Numbers don't tell the whole story. Dive into the qualitative feedback:

1. Review user comments and suggestions
2. Analyze patterns in reported issues
3. Consider any observed usability challenges

Quantitative metrics may indicate success while qualitative feedback uncovers critical usability issues frustrating users. Both data types are essential for a complete understanding of user experience!

Go/No-Go Decision

Based on your analysis, it's time for the big decision: is the software ready for release?

Consider:

1. Have all critical and high-priority issues been resolved?
2. Are users able to complete key workflows without significant problems?
3. Does the software meet the defined acceptance criteria?
4. Are there any showstopper issues that must be addressed before release?

This decision often involves stakeholders beyond the development team. Present your findings clearly and be prepared to make recommendations.

Post-UAT Activities

Congratulations! You've made it through UAT. But before you pop that champagne, there are a few crucial post-UAT activities to wrap up.

Finalizing Documentation

Update your project documentation based on UAT findings:

1. User manuals and help documentation
2. Known issues and workarounds
3. FAQs based on common user questions during UAT

Training and Support Preparation

Prepare your support team:

1. Share insights from UAT to help them anticipate user questions
2. Update training materials based on UAT feedback
3. Consider creating quick-start guides for common tasks

Lessons Learned

Conduct a retrospective to capture lessons learned:

1. What went well in the UAT process?
2. What could be improved for next time?
3. Were there any surprises that could have been anticipated?

Retrospectives often uncover critical insights—like test cases being too technical for users—leading to significant improvements in UAT processes. Continuous reflection helps refine testing approaches for better outcomes.

Conclusion

User Acceptance Testing is more than just a final checkbox in your development process. It's your opportunity to see your software through the eyes of your users, to validate that what you've built truly meets their needs and expectations.

Remember, UAT is not about achieving perfection. It's about ensuring your software is ready to provide value to your users in the real world. Embrace the feedback, learn from the process, and use these insights to continually improve your software and your development practices.

As we wrap up this chapter, I hope you feel equipped and excited to embark on your UAT journey. In our next chapter, we'll explore the critical phase of deployment planning, where we'll take all the insights gained from UAT and prepare to launch your software into the world. Get ready to turn your user-accepted software into user-loved software!

Chapter 13: Deployment Planning

Introduction

Welcome to the exciting world of deployment planning! If you've made it this far in your software development journey, you're on the cusp of bringing your creation to life. But before we pop the champagne, we need to ensure a smooth transition from development to production. That's where deployment planning comes in.

Major deployments require meticulous preparation, similar to a space launch, with comprehensive checklists and thorough validation. Last-minute oversights can lead to critical failures, making structured deployment planning essential for success.

In this chapter, we'll explore the three pillars of successful deployment:

1. Release management processes
2. Deployment checklist and readiness assessment
3. Rollback strategies

By the end of this chapter, you'll have the knowledge and tools to confidently plan and execute your deployments. So, let's strap in and prepare for launch!

Release Management Processes

The Importance of a Structured Release Process

Think of release management as the conductor of an orchestra. Without it, you'd have chaos – instruments playing out of sync, missed cues, and a very unhappy audience. In the world of software deployment, a well-structured release process ensures that all components of your software symphony come together harmoniously.

Without a proper release management process, deployments become chaotic—developers push code inconsistently, versioning is unclear, and documentation suffers. This leads to unreliable releases and operational headaches, underscoring the necessity of implementing structured release management practices.

Key Components of Release Management

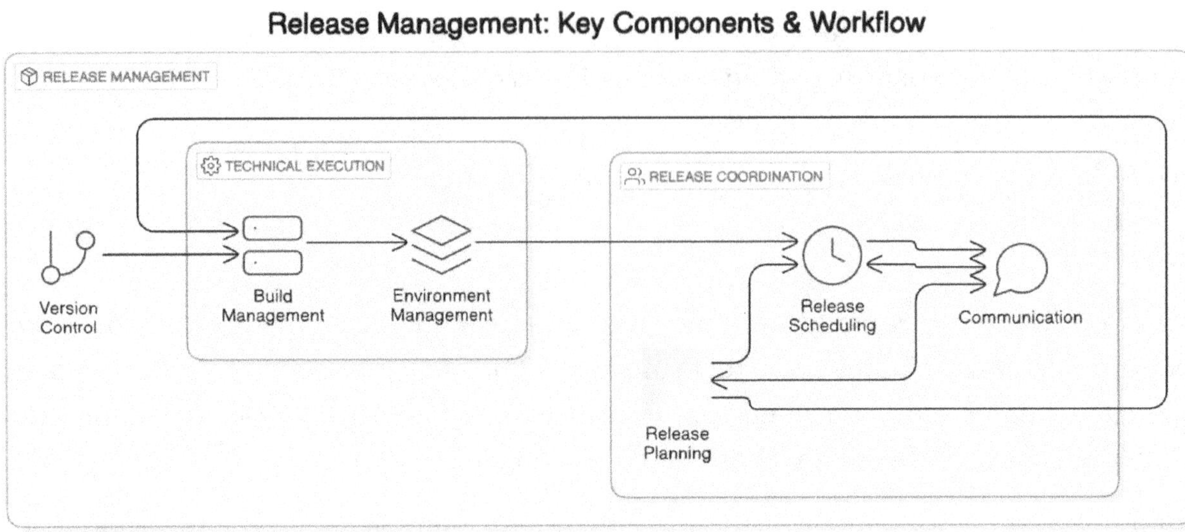

Version Control: This is your sheet music. It keeps track of all changes made to your codebase and allows you to roll back if needed. Tools like Git are essential for managing your code versions effectively.

1. **Release Planning**: Just as a conductor plans which pieces to perform in a concert, you need to plan what features and fixes will go into each release. This involves prioritizing tasks, estimating timelines, and coordinating with various teams.
2. **Build Management**: This is where you assemble all the components of your software. Automated build tools like Jenkins or Travis CI can help ensure consistency and reduce human error.
3. **Environment Management**: You wouldn't practice a symphony in the concert hall. Similarly, you need separate environments for development, testing, and production. Each environment should be as similar as possible to avoid the dreaded "but it worked on my machine" scenario.
4. **Release Scheduling**: Timing is everything. Choose your release dates carefully, considering factors like user impact, team availability, and business priorities.
5. **Communication**: Keep all stakeholders informed about the release process. This includes developers, testers, operations teams, and end-users. Clear

communication can prevent misunderstandings and ensure everyone is on the same page.

Implementing a Release Management Process

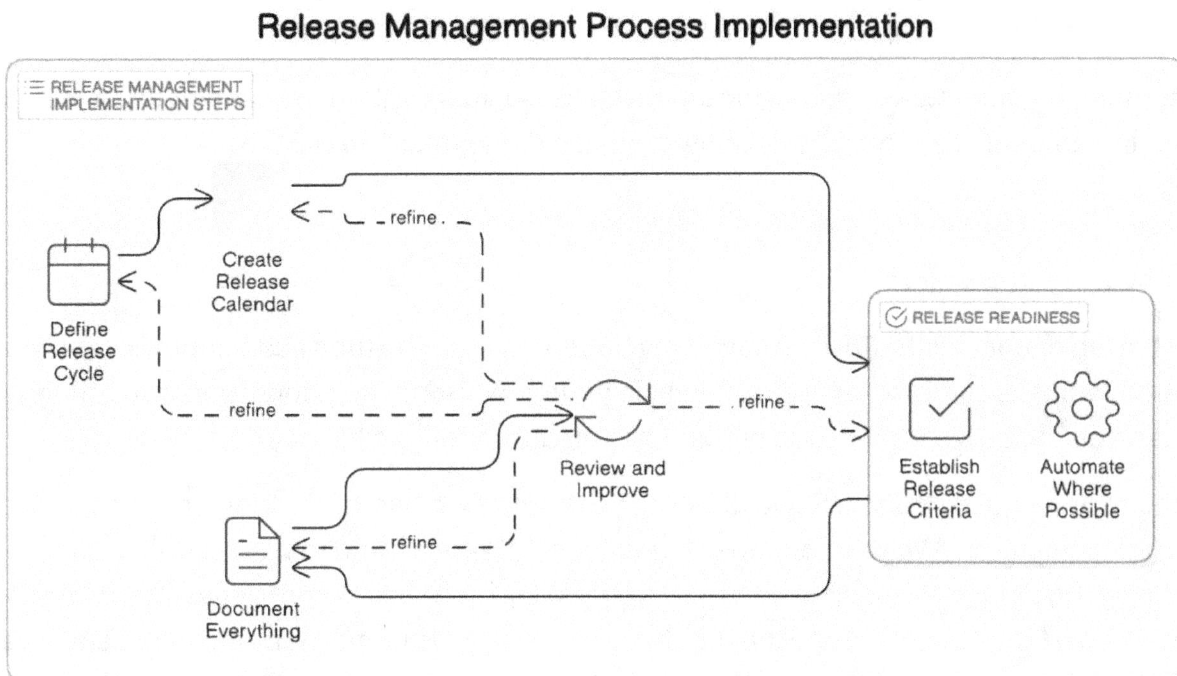

Now that we've covered the key components, let's talk about how to implement a release management process in your organization:

1. **Define Your Release Cycle**: Decide how often you want to release new versions of your software. This could be weekly, monthly, quarterly, or any other interval that makes sense for your project.

2. **Create a Release Calendar**: Map out your releases for the year (or whatever timeframe makes sense). This helps teams plan their work and sets clear expectations for stakeholders.

3. **Establish Release Criteria**: What conditions need to be met before a release can go live? This might include passing all tests, obtaining necessary approvals, or completing user documentation.

4. **Automate Where Possible**: The more you can automate in your release process, the more consistent and reliable it will be. Look for opportunities to automate builds, tests, and even parts of the deployment itself.

5. **Document Everything**: Create clear, detailed documentation for your release process. This should include step-by-step instructions, checklists, and contact information for key personnel.
6. **Review and Improve**: After each release, conduct a retrospective. What went well? What could be improved? Use these insights to continually refine your process.

Remember, a good release management process is like a well-oiled machine. It takes time to set up, but once it's running smoothly, it makes deployments a breeze.

Deployment Checklist and Readiness Assessment

The Power of Checklists

I'm a big fan of checklists. They've saved my bacon more times than I can count. In the world of deployment, a comprehensive checklist is your best friend. It ensures you don't miss any crucial steps and gives you peace of mind as you approach the big day.

Let me share a quick story. On one project, we thought we had everything under control for a major deployment. We were confident, maybe a little too confident. We didn't bother with a formal checklist because, hey, we were pros, right? Well, come deployment day, we realized we'd forgotten to update the database schema. Cue panic, frantic coding, and a very long night. From that day on, I vowed never to underestimate the power of a good checklist.

Creating Your Deployment Checklist

Your deployment checklist will be unique to your project, but here are some key areas you should consider including:

1. **Code Readiness**
    - All features complete and tested
    - Code reviews completed
    - All unit tests passing
    - Integration tests passing
    - Performance tests completed
2. **Environment Preparation**
    - Production environment configured
    - Necessary hardware/cloud resources allocated

- Required third-party services or APIs configured
- Database prepared (including any necessary migrations)

3. **Documentation**
    - Release notes prepared
    - User documentation updated
    - API documentation (if applicable) updated
    - Internal documentation updated
4. **Backup and Recovery**
    - Production data backed up
    - Rollback plan in place and tested
5. **Security**
    - Security audits completed
    - Vulnerabilities addressed
    - Access controls reviewed and updated
6. **Performance**
    - Load testing completed
    - Scalability tested
    - Monitoring tools in place
7. **Compliance and Legal**
    - Necessary legal approvals obtained
    - Compliance requirements met (e.g., GDPR, HIPAA)
8. **Stakeholder Communication**
    - Users notified of upcoming changes
    - Support team briefed on new features/changes
    - Management sign-off obtained
9. **Post-Deployment**

- Smoke tests prepared
- Monitoring alerts configured
- On-call schedule established

Remember, this is a starting point. Tailor your checklist to your specific needs and keep refining it based on your experiences.

Conducting a Readiness Assessment

Deployment Readiness Assessment Process

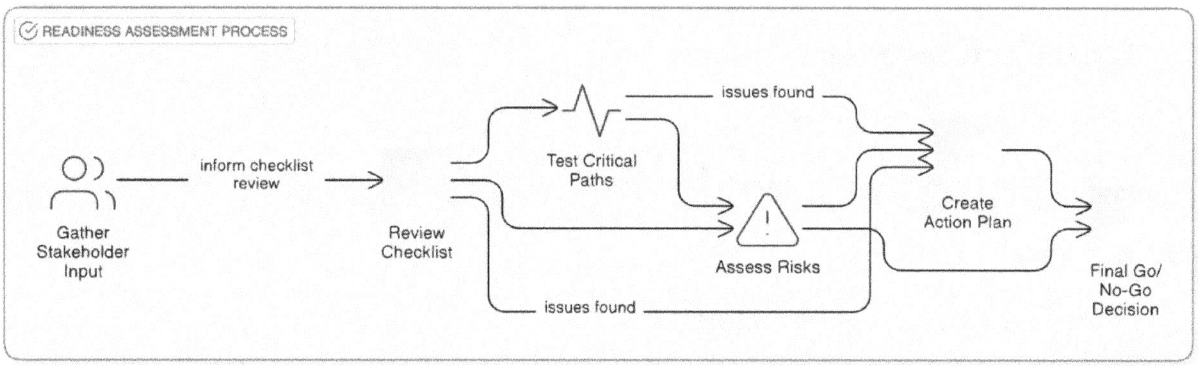

A readiness assessment is like a dress rehearsal for your deployment. It's your chance to identify any gaps or issues before the real thing. Here's how to conduct an effective readiness assessment:

1. **Review the Checklist**: Go through your deployment checklist item by item. For each item, assign a status (e.g., Complete, In Progress, Not Started) and note any issues or concerns.
2. **Gather Stakeholder Input**: Don't rely solely on your own assessment. Consult with team members, including developers, testers, operations staff, and business stakeholders. They may spot issues you've overlooked.
3. **Test Critical Paths**: Identify the most critical aspects of your deployment (e.g., data migration, key functionality) and give these extra attention. Consider running a mock deployment in a staging environment.
4. **Assess Risks**: For any items that aren't fully complete or have known issues, assess the potential impact. Is it a showstopper, or something that can be addressed post-deployment?
5. **Create an Action Plan**: For any issues identified, create a plan to address them. Assign owners and deadlines to ensure everything is resolved before deployment day.

6. **Final Go/No-Go Decision**: Based on your assessment, make a final decision on whether to proceed with the deployment. Don't be afraid to delay if significant issues are uncovered – it's better to get it right than to rush and face bigger problems later.

By thoroughly going through this process, you'll dramatically increase your chances of a smooth, successful deployment. And trust me, there's no better feeling than watching a well-planned deployment unfold without a hitch.

Rollback Strategies

The Importance of Having an Escape Hatch

Let's talk about rollback strategies, or as I like to call them, your deployment parachute. No matter how well you plan, how thoroughly you test, there's always a chance that something could go wrong in production. That's where your rollback strategy comes in.

Failed deployments without rollback plans can escalate into system-wide outages, turning quick reversions into hours of crisis management. This highlights the critical need for pre-tested, reliable rollback strategies in every release plan to ensure rapid recovery when issues arise.

Types of Rollback Strategies

Rollback Strategies Comparison

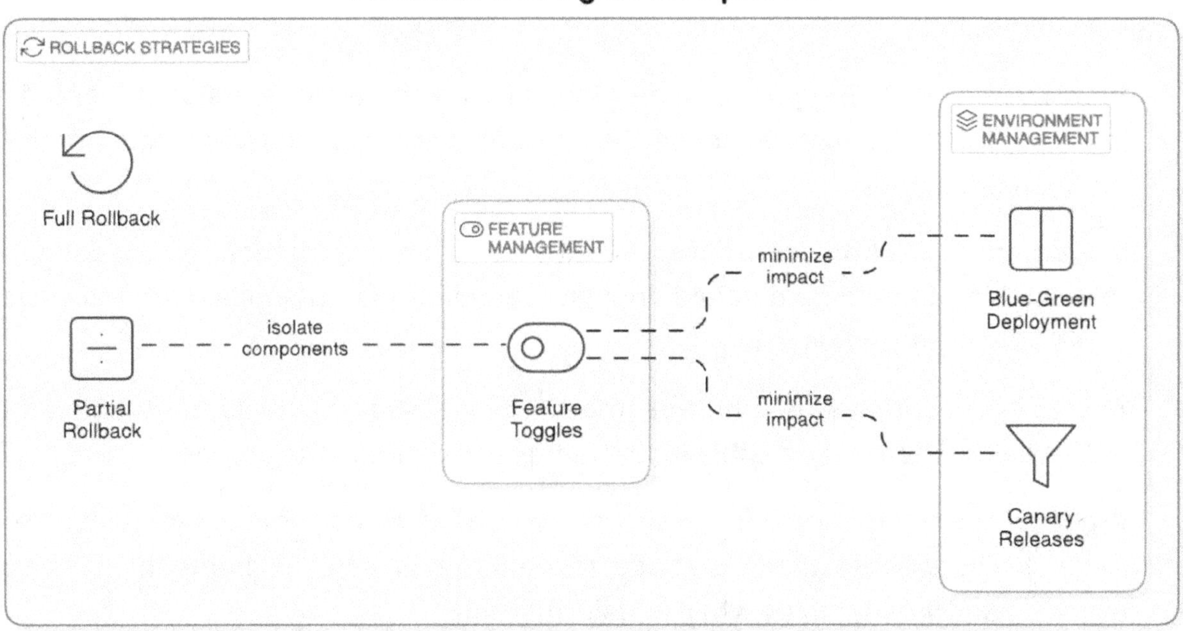

There are several approaches to rolling back a deployment. The best choice depends on your specific situation, but here are some common strategies:

1. **Full Rollback**: This involves completely reverting to the previous version of your software. It's the most straightforward approach but can be time-consuming for large systems.
2. **Partial Rollback**: In this approach, you only roll back the specific components that are causing issues. This can be faster than a full rollback but requires careful planning and the ability to isolate components.
3. **Feature Toggles**: By using feature toggles (also known as feature flags), you can quickly disable problematic features without rolling back the entire deployment. This is a great option for isolating issues and maintaining stability.
4. **Blue-Green Deployment**: In this strategy, you maintain two identical production environments. One (blue) runs the current version, while the other (green) runs the new version. If issues arise, you can quickly switch traffic back to the blue environment.
5. **Canary Releases**: Similar to blue-green, but instead of switching all traffic, you gradually route users to the new version. If problems occur, you can easily route users back to the old version.

Developing Your Rollback Strategy

Now that we've covered the types of rollback strategies, let's talk about how to develop an effective rollback plan:

1. **Identify Rollback Triggers**: Define clear criteria for when a rollback should be initiated. This might include specific error rates, performance thresholds, or critical functionality failures.
2. **Document the Rollback Process**: Create step-by-step instructions for executing the rollback. This should be detailed enough that someone unfamiliar with the system could follow them if necessary.
3. **Assign Roles and Responsibilities**: Clearly define who has the authority to initiate a rollback and who is responsible for executing each step of the process.
4. **Practice the Rollback**: Don't wait until you have a real emergency to test your rollback strategy. Regularly practice rollbacks in a safe environment to ensure everyone knows what to do when it really matters.
5. **Automate Where Possible**: The more you can automate your rollback process, the faster and more reliable it will be. Consider using scripts or deployment tools that can quickly revert changes.

6. **Plan for Data**: If your deployment involves database changes, make sure your rollback strategy accounts for reverting these changes without losing data.

7. **Communicate**: Ensure all stakeholders know about the rollback plan and what to expect if it needs to be executed. This includes internal teams and, if necessary, end-users.

Executing a Rollback

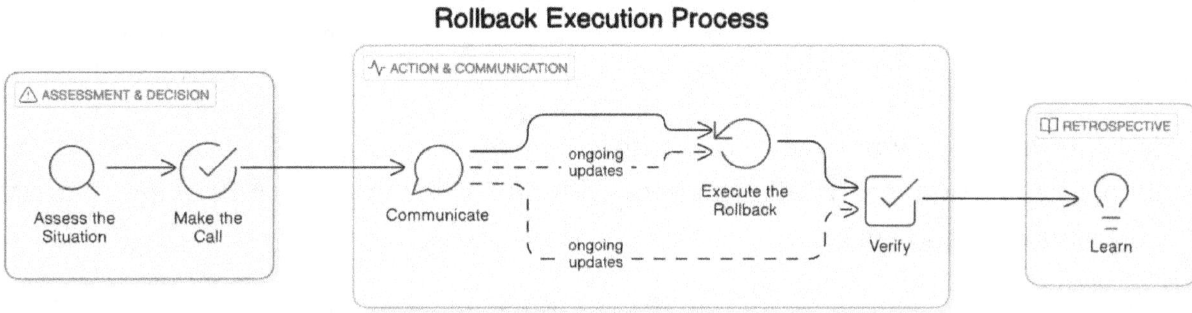

If you find yourself in a situation where you need to execute a rollback, here's a general process to follow:

1. **Assess the Situation**: Quickly gather information about the issue. Is it affecting all users or just a subset? Is it a critical failure or a minor bug?

2. **Make the Call**: Based on your predefined triggers and the current situation, decide whether to initiate the rollback.

3. **Communicate**: Notify all relevant parties that a rollback is in progress. This might include your development team, support staff, and end-users.

4. **Execute the Rollback**: Follow your documented rollback process step by step. Don't skip steps, even if you think you know what you're doing – stress can make even experienced professionals forget crucial details.

5. **Verify**: Once the rollback is complete, thoroughly test the system to ensure it's functioning correctly and the issue has been resolved.

6. **Learn**: After things have calmed down, conduct a post-mortem. What went wrong? How can you prevent similar issues in the future? Use these insights to improve both your deployment and rollback processes.

Remember, a good rollback strategy is like an insurance policy. You hope you never have to use it, but you'll be incredibly glad it's there if you need it.

Conclusion

As we wrap up this chapter on deployment planning, I hope you're feeling more confident about tackling your next deployment. We've covered a lot of ground, from establishing a solid release management process to creating comprehensive deployment checklists and developing robust rollback strategies.

Remember, successful deployments don't happen by accident. They're the result of careful planning, thorough preparation, and a healthy dose of caution. By implementing the strategies we've discussed, you'll be well on your way to smoother, more reliable deployments.

But don't stop here. Deployment planning is an ongoing process. Keep refining your approach, learning from each deployment (successful or otherwise), and staying up to date with new tools and techniques.

As you move forward, keep in mind that deployment is just one part of the larger picture of continuous delivery and deployment. In the next chapter, we'll explore how to take your deployment game to the next level with continuous deployment and delivery practices. Get ready to dive into the world of CI/CD pipelines, automated deployment tools, and the cutting-edge techniques that are shaping the future of software delivery.

Until then, happy deploying!

Chapter 14: Continuous Deployment and Delivery

Introduction

Welcome to the exciting world of Continuous Deployment and Delivery! If you've been following along with our journey through the Software Development Life Cycle (SDLC), you're probably eager to see your hard work come to fruition. Well, you're in luck because that's exactly what we're going to explore in this chapter.

I remember the first time I implemented a CI/CD pipeline in my team. It was like watching a well-oiled machine come to life. Gone were the days of manual deployments and crossed fingers. Instead, we had a smooth, automated process that allowed us to deliver value to our users faster than ever before. Trust me, once you experience the power of Continuous Deployment and Delivery, you'll wonder how you ever managed without it.

In this chapter, we'll dive deep into the world of CI/CD pipelines, explore automated deployment tools and scripts, and uncover the magic of feature flags and canary releases. So, buckle up and get ready for an exciting ride!

Chapter 14: Continuous Deployment and Delivery

Setting Up Your CI/CD Pipeline

Understanding CI/CD

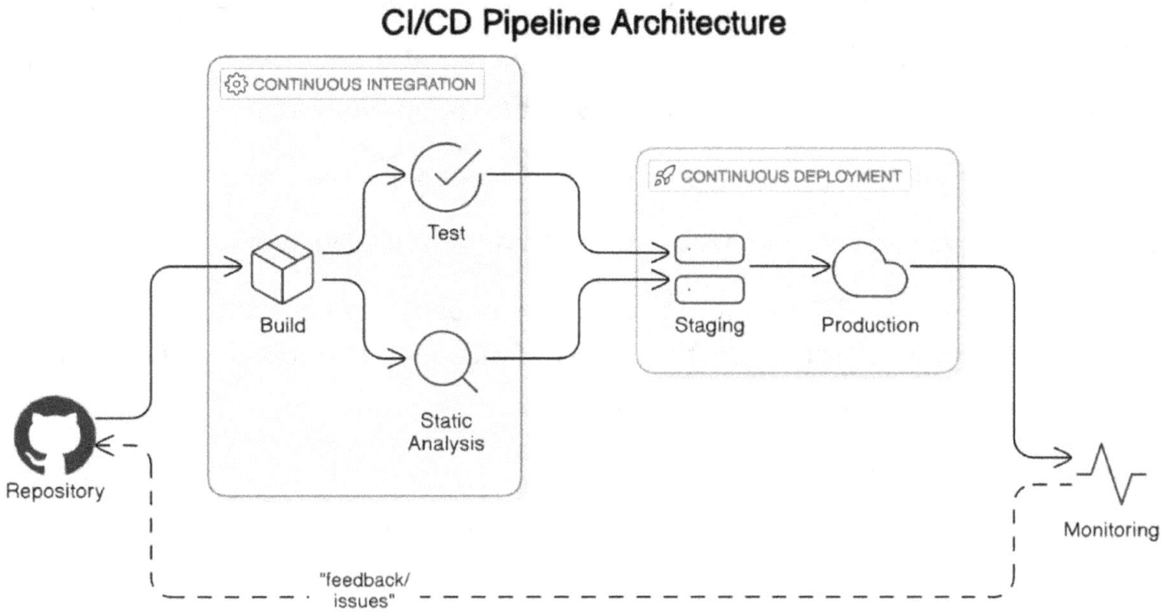

Before we roll up our sleeves and start building, let's make sure we're on the same page about what CI/CD actually means. CI stands for Continuous Integration, and CD can stand for either Continuous Delivery or Continuous Deployment. Confused yet? Don't worry, I've got you covered.

Continuous Integration is the practice of regularly merging code changes into a central repository, after which automated builds and tests are run. The goal here is to catch and fix integration issues early in the development process.

Continuous Delivery takes this a step further. It's an approach where teams ensure that the code is always in a deployable state, even if they're not deploying it immediately.

Continuous Deployment is the final frontier. It's like Continuous Delivery on steroids, where every change that passes all stages of your production pipeline is released to your customers. There's no human intervention, and only a failed test will prevent a new change from being deployed to production.

Choosing Your CI/CD Tools

Now that we understand what CI/CD is, let's talk about the tools we can use to implement it. There are many options out there, and choosing the right one can feel overwhelming. But don't worry, I've been there, and I'm here to help guide you through it.

Some popular CI/CD tools include:

1. Jenkins: An open-source automation server that offers a wide range of plugins.
2. GitLab CI/CD: Integrated with GitLab, making it a great choice if you're already using GitLab for source control.
3. Travis CI: Known for its ease of use and great for open-source projects.
4. CircleCI: Offers a cloud-based solution with a focus on speed and efficiency.
5. Azure DevOps: Microsoft's offering, which integrates well with other Microsoft tools.

When I first started with CI/CD, I went with Jenkins because of its flexibility and the wealth of resources available online. But the best tool for you will depend on your specific needs, your team's expertise, and your existing infrastructure.

Setting Up Your First Pipeline

Let's walk through setting up a basic CI/CD pipeline using Jenkins. Don't worry if you're using a different tool; the principles remain the same.

1. Install Jenkins: First, you'll need to install Jenkins on a server. You can download it from the official Jenkins website and follow their installation guide.
2. Create a New Job: In Jenkins, click on "New Item" to create a new job. Give it a name and select "Pipeline" as the job type.
3. Configure Source Control: In the job configuration, set up your source control. If you're using Git, you'll need to provide the repository URL and credentials.
4. Write Your Pipeline Script: Jenkins uses a domain-specific language called Jenkinsfile to define pipelines. Here's a simple example:

```
pipeline {
  agent any
  stages {
    stage('Build') {
      steps {
        sh 'npm install'
        sh 'npm run build'
      }
    }
    stage('Test') {
      steps {
        sh 'npm test'
```

```
        }
      }
      stage('Deploy') {
        steps {
          sh 'npm run deploy'
        }
      }
    }
  }
```

This pipeline has three stages: Build, Test, and Deploy. Each stage runs specific shell commands.

5. Save and Run: Save your configuration and run the pipeline. Jenkins will now automatically execute these steps whenever changes are pushed to your repository.

Remember, this is just a basic example. As you become more comfortable with CI/CD, you'll likely want to add more stages, incorporate more sophisticated testing, and implement approval processes for production deployments.

Automated Deployment Tools and Scripts

Now that we have our CI/CD pipeline set up, let's talk about automating the deployment process itself. After all, the whole point of Continuous Deployment is to get your code from your repository to your production environment quickly and reliably.

Configuration Management Tools

Configuration management tools are a key component of automated deployments. They allow you to define your infrastructure as code, ensuring consistency across environments and making it easy to replicate your setup.

Some popular configuration management tools include:

1. Ansible: Known for its simplicity and agentless architecture.
2. Puppet: Offers a declarative language for describing system configurations.
3. Chef: Uses a domain-specific language based on Ruby.

I've had great experiences with Ansible. Its YAML-based playbooks are easy to read and write, and it doesn't require any agents to be installed on the target machines.

Here's a simple Ansible playbook that deploys a Node.js application:

```
---
- hosts: webservers
  tasks:
    - name: Clone the repository
      git:
        repo: 'https://github.com/yourusername/yourrepo.git'
        dest: /var/www/myapp

    - name: Install dependencies
      npm:
        path: /var/www/myapp

    - name: Start the application
      command: npm start
      args:
        chdir: /var/www/myapp
```

This playbook clones a Git repository, installs the necessary dependencies, and starts the application.

Containerization and Orchestration

In recent years, containerization has revolutionized the way we deploy applications. Docker, the most popular containerization platform, allows you to package your application and all its dependencies into a standardized unit called a container.

But managing multiple containers across multiple hosts can be challenging. That's where container orchestration tools like Kubernetes come in. Kubernetes automates the deployment, scaling, and management of containerized applications.

Here's a simple example of a Kubernetes deployment configuration:

```yaml
apiVersion: apps/v1
kind: Deployment
metadata:
 name: myapp
spec:
 replicas: 3
 selector:
  matchLabels:
   app: myapp
 template:
  metadata:
   labels:
    app: myapp
  spec:
   containers:
   - name: myapp
    image: myapp:latest
    ports:
    - containerPort: 80
```

This configuration tells Kubernetes to create three replicas of your application, each running in its own container.

Scripting Your Deployments

While tools like Ansible and Kubernetes are powerful, sometimes you might need to write custom scripts to handle specific deployment tasks. These scripts can be written in any language you're comfortable with, but shell scripts are a common choice due to their ubiquity on Unix-like systems.

Here's a simple bash script that deploys a Node.js application:

```bash
#!/bin/bash

# Pull the latest changes
git pull origin master

# Install dependencies
npm install

# Build the application
npm run build

# Restart the application
pm2 restart myapp
```

This script pulls the latest changes from Git, installs any new dependencies, builds the application, and then restarts it using the process manager PM2.

Feature Flags and Canary Releases

Now that we've covered the basics of automated deployments, let's talk about some advanced techniques that can make your deployments even safer and more flexible.

Feature Flags

Feature flags (also known as feature toggles) are a powerful technique that allows you to modify system behavior without changing code. They're particularly useful in a Continuous Deployment environment because they allow you to deploy code to production that isn't yet ready for all users.

Here's a simple example of a feature flag in JavaScript:

```javascript
if (featureFlags.newFeature) {
  // New feature code
```

```
} else {
  // Old feature code
}
```

In this example, featureFlags.newFeature could be controlled by a configuration file or a database, allowing you to turn the feature on or off without redeploying your application.

Feature flags can be used for:

1. A/B testing: Compare two versions of a feature to see which performs better.
2. Gradual rollouts: Slowly increase the number of users who have access to a new feature.
3. Canary releases: Test a new feature with a small subset of users before a full rollout.
4. Emergency killswitches: Quickly disable a problematic feature without rolling back the entire deployment.

Feature flags enable gradual rollouts of major changes—like UI redesigns—starting with a small user subset and scaling up based on feedback. This approach minimizes risk by isolating issues and allowing iterative improvements before full deployment.

Canary Releases

Canary releases are a technique for reducing the risk of introducing a new software version in production by slowly rolling out the change to a small subset of users before rolling it out to the entire infrastructure and making it available to everybody.

The term "canary" comes from the old mining practice of bringing canaries into coal mines. If the canary died, it was an early warning sign of toxic gases, telling the miners to evacuate.

Here's how you might implement a canary release:

1. Deploy the new version to a small subset of your servers (say, 5%).
2. Route a small percentage of your traffic to these servers.
3. Monitor the performance and error rates closely.
4. If everything looks good, gradually increase the percentage of traffic going to the new version.
5. If issues are detected, quickly route all traffic back to the old version.

Canary releases can be implemented using your load balancer or a service mesh like Istio. Here's a simple example using Nginx:

```
upstream backend {
  server old-version.example.com weight=95;
  server new-version.example.com weight=5;
}
server {
  listen 80;
  location / {
    proxy_pass http://backend;
  }
}
```

This configuration sends 5% of traffic to the new version and 95% to the old version.

Monitoring and Observability in CI/CD

As we wrap up our discussion on Continuous Deployment and Delivery, it's crucial to touch on the importance of monitoring and observability. When you're deploying frequently, potentially multiple times a day, you need to be able to quickly detect and respond to any issues that arise.

Implementing Effective Monitoring

Monitoring is all about collecting and analyzing metrics from your systems to ensure they're operating as expected. In a CI/CD environment, you should be monitoring:

1. System metrics: CPU usage, memory usage, disk I/O, network traffic.
2. Application metrics: Response times, error rates, request rates.
3. Business metrics: User signups, transactions, active users.

Tools like Prometheus, Grafana, and ELK stack (Elasticsearch, Logstash, and Kibana) can help you collect and visualize these metrics.

Here's a simple example of how you might use Prometheus to monitor a Node.js application:

```
const express = require('express');
const prometheus = require('prom-client');

const app = express();

// Create a counter metric
const httpRequestsTotal = new prometheus.Counter({
  name: 'http_requests_total',
  help: 'Total number of HTTP requests',
  labelNames: ['method', 'route', 'status']
});

// Middleware to increment the counter
app.use((req, res, next) => {
  res.on('finish', () => {
    httpRequestsTotal.inc({
      method: req.method,
      route: req.route.path,
      status: res.statusCode
    });
  });
  next();
});

// Expose metrics endpoint
```

```
app.get('/metrics', async (req, res) => {
  res.set('Content-Type', prometheus.register.contentType);
  res.end(await prometheus.register.metrics());
});

app.listen(3000);
```

This code sets up a counter to track HTTP requests and exposes a /metrics endpoint that Prometheus can scrape.

Enhancing Observability

While monitoring gives you an overview of your system's health, observability goes a step further. It's about having enough context to understand why your system is behaving the way it is.

Key components of observability include:

1. Logging: Detailed records of events in your system.
2. Tracing: Following a request as it moves through your system.
3. Metrics: Numerical measurements of your system over time.

Tools like Jaeger for tracing and Loki for logging can complement your monitoring setup to provide full observability.

Here's an example of how you might add tracing to a Node.js application using OpenTelemetry:

```
const opentelemetry = require('@opentelemetry/api');
const { NodeTracerProvider } = require('@opentelemetry/node');
const { SimpleSpanProcessor } = require('@opentelemetry/tracing');
const { JaegerExporter } = require('@opentelemetry/exporter-jaeger');

const provider = new NodeTracerProvider();
```

```
const exporter = new JaegerExporter({
  serviceName: 'my-service',
});

provider.addSpanProcessor(new SimpleSpanProcessor(exporter));

provider.register();

const tracer = opentelemetry.trace.getTracer('example-basic-tracer-node');

// Your application code here
const span = tracer.startSpan('main');
for (let i = 0; i < 10; i++) {
  doWork(i);
}
span.end();

function doWork(i) {
  const span = tracer.startSpan('doWork');
  // Simulate some work
  for (let j = 0; j < 1000000; j++) {}
  span.end();
}
```

This code sets up a basic tracer that will send span data to Jaeger, allowing you to visualize the flow of requests through your application.

Chapter 14: Continuous Deployment and Delivery

Conclusion

Congratulations! You've made it through our deep dive into Continuous Deployment and Delivery. We've covered a lot of ground, from setting up CI/CD pipelines to implementing advanced techniques like feature flags and canary releases.

Remember, implementing CI/CD is a journey, not a destination. Start small, perhaps with a non-critical application, and gradually expand your CI/CD practices as you become more comfortable. Always keep learning and refining your processes.

As we wrap up, I want to share a personal anecdote. When I first implemented CI/CD in my team, we faced a lot of resistance. People were worried about the risks of automatic deployments and the effort required to set everything up. But after a few months, even the biggest skeptics were convinced. Our deployment frequency increased, our error rates decreased, and most importantly, we were delivering value to our users faster than ever before.

So, don't be discouraged if you face challenges along the way. The benefits of Continuous Deployment and Delivery are well worth the effort. Keep pushing forward, and before you know it, you'll be deploying with confidence multiple times a day.

In our next chapter, we'll explore the fascinating world of Blue-Green Deployment Strategy. This technique will add another layer of safety to your deployment process, allowing you to switch between different versions of your application with zero downtime. So, stay tuned and happy deploying!

Chapter 15: Blue-Green Deployment Strategy

Introduction

Welcome to the exciting world of blue-green deployments! If you've ever felt the anxiety of pushing updates to your production environment, wondering if something might go wrong and leave your users stranded, then this chapter is for you. I've been there, and I know that feeling all too well. But fear not! Blue-green deployment is here to save the day, and I'm going to walk you through everything you need to know to master this powerful technique.

Think of blue-green deployment as having a safety net for your software releases. It's like being a trapeze artist with a second trapeze ready to catch you if you miss your grip. In this chapter, we'll explore how to set up that safety net, how to swing from one environment to another seamlessly, and how to make sure you always land on your feet.

Understanding Blue-Green Deployment

Before we dive into the nitty-gritty, let's get a clear picture of what blue-green deployment actually is. Imagine you have two identical production environments: one we'll call "blue" and the other "green." At any given time, only one of these environments is live and serving your users. The other sits idle, waiting for its moment to shine.

When it's time to deploy a new version of your application, you don't update the live environment directly. Instead, you update the idle environment. Once you're confident that everything is working correctly in the updated environment, you simply switch the traffic from the old environment to the new one. Voila! Your new version is live, and if anything goes wrong, you can switch back to the old version in seconds.

Blue-green deployments provide a reliable strategy for updating high-traffic systems, eliminating downtime risks with instant rollback capabilities. This approach is particularly valuable for mission-critical applications requiring uninterrupted availability.

Blue-Green Deployment in Microservices Architecture

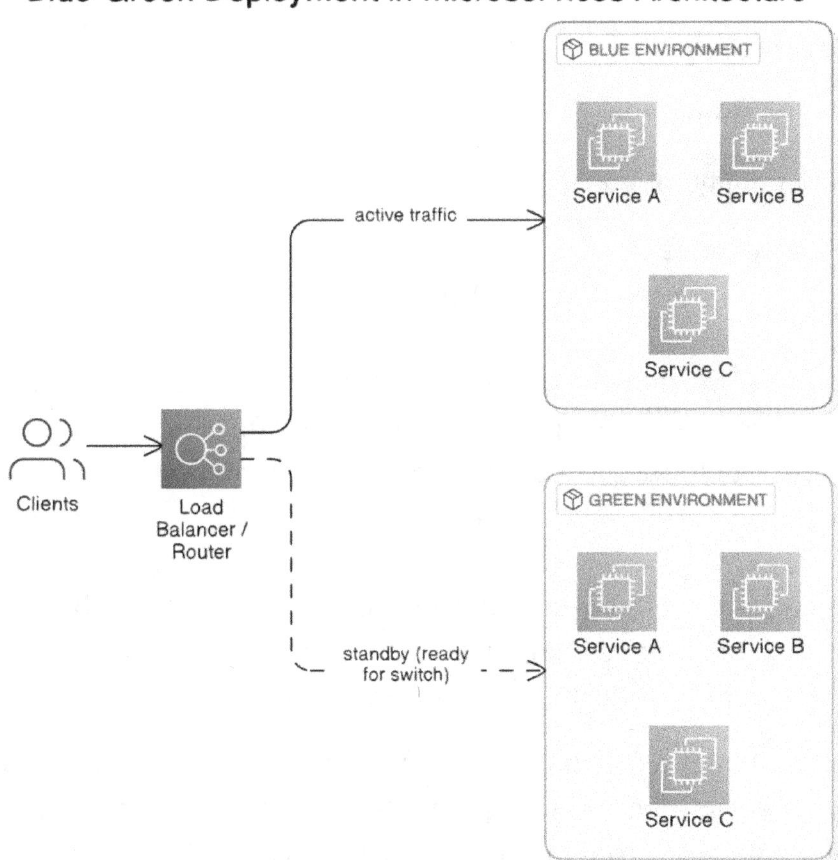

Infrastructure Setup for Blue-Green Deployments

Now that you understand the concept, let's talk about how to set up your infrastructure to support blue-green deployments. This is where the magic happens, and it's crucial to get it right.

Identical Environments

The first step is to create two identical production environments. When I say identical, I mean down to the last detail. Same hardware specifications, same software versions, same configuration – everything. This ensures that your application will behave the same way in both environments.

Here's a checklist to help you ensure your environments are truly identical:

1. Server specifications (CPU, RAM, storage)
2. Operating system version and patches
3. Runtime environments (e.g., Java JDK, Node.js version)
4. Database systems and versions
5. Caching layers (e.g., Redis, Memcached)
6. Load balancers and their configurations
7. Network settings and firewall rules
8. Monitoring and logging tools

I once worked on a project where we thought our environments were identical, only to discover a slight difference in the database configuration that caused unexpected behavior in one environment. Trust me, you don't want to learn this lesson the hard way!

Automation is Key

To make blue-green deployments truly effective, you need to automate as much of the process as possible. This includes provisioning new environments, deploying your application, running tests, and switching traffic between environments.

Tools like Terraform, Ansible, or CloudFormation can be invaluable for infrastructure-as-code, allowing you to define your environments in a repeatable, version-controlled manner. For application deployment, consider using tools like Jenkins, GitLab CI, or CircleCI to create automated pipelines.

Here's a simple example of how your deployment pipeline might look:

1. Trigger deployment to the idle environment
2. Run automated tests in the idle environment
3. If tests pass, update DNS or load balancer to point to the new environment
4. Run smoke tests to verify the switch was successful
5. If any issues are detected, automatically roll back to the previous environment

Remember, the goal is to make the deployment process as smooth and error-free as possible. The more you can automate, the less room there is for human error.

Traffic Routing and Load Balancing

One of the most critical aspects of blue-green deployment is how you handle traffic routing. After all, the whole point is to seamlessly direct your users from the old version to the new version without them even noticing.

DNS-based Routing

One approach is to use DNS-based routing. In this scenario, you update your DNS records to point to the IP address of the new environment when you're ready to switch. This method is relatively simple but comes with a caveat: DNS propagation can take time, sometimes up to 24 hours, depending on TTL (Time to Live) settings.

Phased rollouts require careful advance planning and can result in temporary version fragmentation, where users simultaneously experience different releases. This approach demands strategic coordination to manage the transition period effectively.

Load Balancer Routing

A more sophisticated and immediate approach is to use a load balancer. With this method, your DNS always points to the load balancer, and you configure the load balancer to direct traffic to either the blue or green environment.

Popular cloud providers offer load balancing solutions that make this process relatively straightforward:

- Amazon Web Services (AWS): Elastic Load Balancing
- Google Cloud Platform (GCP): Cloud Load Balancing
- Microsoft Azure: Azure Load Balancer

Using a load balancer gives you instantaneous control over traffic routing. You can switch all traffic at once or gradually shift traffic from one environment to another, which brings us to our next topic.

Gradual Traffic Shifting

Sometimes, you might want to gradually shift traffic from the old environment to the new one. This approach, often called "traffic shaping" or "canary releasing," allows you to test the new version with a small percentage of your users before fully committing.

Here's how you might implement gradual traffic shifting:

1. Start by routing 10% of traffic to the new environment
2. Monitor for any errors or performance issues
3. If everything looks good, increase to 25%, then 50%, and so on
4. If issues arise, you can quickly revert to the old environment

Canary deployments serve as a crucial safety net for critical updates, uncovering real-world issues that testing environments might miss before full rollout. This method provides an essential layer of protection against production failures.

Monitoring and Rollback Procedures

No matter how well you plan and test, there's always a chance something could go wrong after deployment. That's why robust monitoring and a solid rollback strategy are essential components of any blue-green deployment setup.

Comprehensive Monitoring

When it comes to monitoring, more is generally better. You want to keep an eye on every aspect of your application and infrastructure. Here are some key metrics to watch:

1. Application performance (response times, error rates)
2. Server health (CPU, memory, disk usage)
3. Database performance (query times, connection pool usage)
4. User behavior (conversion rates, session duration)
5. Business metrics (sales, signups, etc.)

Tools like Prometheus, Grafana, New Relic, or Datadog can help you set up comprehensive monitoring dashboards. The key is to have all your critical metrics in one place so you can quickly spot any issues.

Relying solely on application metrics after deployment can mask critical failures—verified only through business metrics that reveal real operational impact. Monitoring both technical and business indicators is essential to detect costly issues that might otherwise go unnoticed.

Automated Alerts

Set up automated alerts for any metrics that deviate from your expected norms. These alerts should be tiered based on severity:

1. Warning alerts for minor issues
2. Critical alerts for major problems
3. Automatic rollback triggers for severe issues

Make sure these alerts go to the right people. There's no point in sending a 3 AM alert to someone who can't do anything about it!

Rollback Procedures

Despite our best efforts, sometimes we need to roll back a deployment. In a blue-green setup, rolling back is as simple as switching traffic back to the old environment. However, you need to consider a few things:

1. Data consistency: If your new version made changes to the database, how will you handle rolling these back?
2. Stateful applications: If your application maintains user sessions, how will you handle active sessions during a rollback?
3. External services: If your new version interacts with external services differently, how will you manage this during a rollback?

Here's a basic rollback procedure you can adapt:

1. Detect the need for a rollback (either through automated alerts or manual decision)
2. Switch traffic back to the old environment
3. Verify that the old environment is functioning correctly
4. Investigate the issue in the new environment

5. Clean up any data inconsistencies if necessary
6. Inform relevant stakeholders about the rollback and its impact

Conducting mock rollback scenarios before major deployments keeps teams prepared and often uncovers overlooked vulnerabilities. This proactive practice ensures smoother recovery if actual rollbacks become necessary.

Best Practices for Blue-Green Deployments

Now that we've covered the main components of blue-green deployment, let's discuss some best practices to help you get the most out of this strategy.

Keep Environments in Sync

Ensure your blue and green environments stay in sync outside of deployment windows. This includes database schemas, configuration files, and any external dependencies. The last thing you want is to switch to your green environment and realize it's missing critical updates.

Automated scripts running regular comparisons between environments can detect discrepancies early, preventing potential issues. This proactive approach helps maintain consistency and reduces troubleshooting efforts!

Test, Test, and Test Again

Before switching traffic to your new environment, run a comprehensive suite of tests. This should include:

1. Unit tests
2. Integration tests
3. End-to-end tests
4. Performance tests
5. Security tests

Don't forget to test your rollback procedure as well. You don't want to be figuring out how to roll back in the middle of a crisis.

Plan for Data Migration

If your new version includes database changes, you need a solid plan for migrating data. This might involve:

1. Running migrations before the switch

2. Using a blue-green database deployment strategy
3. Employing a "copy-on-write" approach for data updates during the transition

Remember, your data migration strategy should also account for potential rollbacks. Always have a way to revert your data to its previous state.

Document Everything

Maintain detailed documentation of your blue-green deployment process. This should include:

1. Environment setup procedures
2. Deployment steps
3. Monitoring guidelines
4. Rollback procedures
5. Lessons learned from previous deployments

Good documentation is invaluable when you're dealing with a critical issue at 2 AM, trust me!

Practice Makes Perfect

Regularly practice your blue-green deployments, including rollbacks. This helps your team become familiar with the process and can reveal potential issues before they become real problems.

"Game days" that simulate deployment scenarios—including worst-case situations—strengthen team preparedness and refine operational processes. These exercises build confidence while identifying areas for improvement in deployment workflows..

Challenges and Considerations

While blue-green deployment is a powerful strategy, it's not without its challenges. Here are a few things to keep in mind:

Cost Implications

Running two production-ready environments can be expensive, especially for smaller organizations. You need to weigh the benefits against the additional infrastructure costs.

Database Considerations

Managing database changes can be tricky in a blue-green setup, especially for applications with high write volumes. You might need to employ advanced techniques like dual writes or read-only replicas during the transition.

Stateful Applications

If your application maintains user sessions or other stateful data, you'll need to devise a strategy for handling this during the switch. This might involve sticky sessions, distributed caching, or other session replication techniques.

External Dependencies

If your application interacts with external services or APIs, ensure that both environments are properly configured and that any necessary credentials or permissions are in place.

Conclusion

Blue-green deployment is a powerful technique that can significantly reduce the risk and downtime associated with software updates. By maintaining two identical production environments and using smart traffic routing, you can achieve near-zero downtime deployments and have the confidence of an instant rollback option.

Remember, the key to successful blue-green deployments lies in careful planning, robust automation, comprehensive monitoring, and regular practice. It may seem like a lot of work upfront, but trust me, the peace of mind it brings is worth every ounce of effort.

As we wrap up this chapter, I hope you're feeling excited about implementing blue-green deployments in your own projects. In the next chapter, we'll explore another powerful deployment strategy: canary releases and A/B testing. These techniques can complement your blue-green setup and provide even more flexibility in how you release new features to your users.

So, are you ready to take the plunge into the world of blue-green deployments? Trust me, once you experience the confidence and control it brings to your release process, you'll wonder how you ever managed without it. Happy deploying!

Chapter 16: Canary Releases and A/B Testing

Introduction to Canary Releases and A/B Testing

Welcome to the exciting world of canary releases and A/B testing! If you've ever wondered how companies like Google, Amazon, or Netflix roll out new features without causing widespread chaos, you're about to find out. In this chapter, we'll dive deep into two powerful techniques that have revolutionized the way we deploy and test software: canary releases and A/B testing.

As a software developer or project manager, you've probably experienced the nail-biting anxiety that comes with pushing a major update to production. Will it work? Will users love it? Or will it crash and burn, leaving you scrambling to fix the mess? Well, I've been there too, and I can tell you that canary releases and A/B testing are game-changers.

Major platform updates deployed without gradual rollouts can lead to immediate system failures, overwhelming customer support and causing revenue loss. This underscores the critical importance of controlled release strategies like canary deployments and A/B testing to mitigate risks!

So, buckle up as we explore these powerful techniques that will help you deploy with confidence, gather real-world data, and make informed decisions about your software updates.

Understanding Canary Releases

What is a Canary Release?

Picture this: you're a coal miner in the early 20th century. Before heading into a potentially dangerous mine shaft, you bring along a canary in a cage. Why? Because canaries are more sensitive to toxic gases than humans. If the canary stops singing or, worse, keels over, you know it's time to get out of there fast!

Now, let's bring this concept into the software world. A canary release is like that sentinel bird, but instead of testing for toxic gases, we're testing new software features or updates. In a canary release, you roll out a new version of your software to a small subset of your users or servers before making it available to everyone.

Gradual deployment strategies allow teams to test new code in production with minimal risk—like testing waters before diving in. This cautious approach provides real-world performance data while limiting potential negative impact.

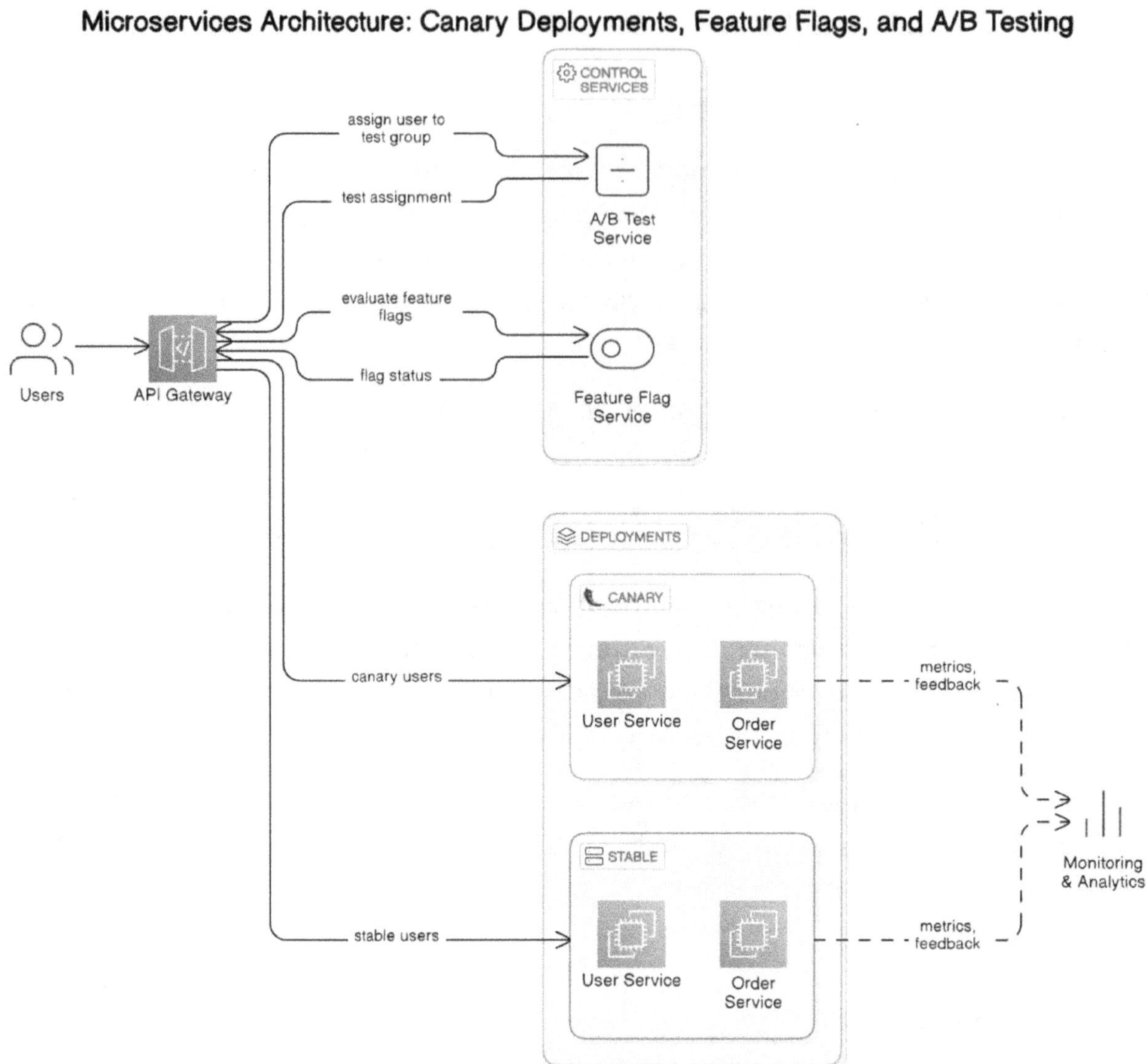

Benefits of Canary Releases

1. **Risk Mitigation**: By limiting the new version to a small group, you minimize the impact of potential bugs or issues.
2. **Real-world Testing**: You get to see how your software performs under actual user conditions, which can reveal issues that might not show up in a controlled test environment.
3. **Gradual Rollout**: If all goes well, you can gradually increase the number of users or servers running the new version, giving you more control over the deployment process.

4. **Quick Rollback**: If something goes wrong, you can quickly revert to the previous version without affecting your entire user base.
5. **User Feedback**: You can gather early feedback from the canary group, which can be invaluable for fine-tuning features or fixing minor issues before a full release.

Implementing Canary Releases

Now that you understand the concept and benefits let's talk about how to implement canary releases in your development process.

1. **Identify Your Canary Group**: This could be a percentage of your users, specific servers, or even a group of beta testers. The key is to choose a representative sample that's small enough to limit risk but large enough to provide meaningful data.
2. **Feature Flags**: Use feature flags in your code to control which users see the new version. This allows you to turn features on and off without redeploying your application.
3. **Monitoring and Metrics**: Set up robust monitoring and define key metrics to track. You'll want to keep a close eye on performance, error rates, and user behavior during the canary release.
4. **Gradual Rollout Plan**: Develop a plan for gradually increasing the canary group size if things go well. This might look something like: 5% -> 10% -> 25% -> 50% -> 100%.
5. **Rollback Strategy**: Have a clear plan for rolling back the changes if issues arise. This should be a quick, automated process to minimize downtime or user impact.

Let me share an example from my own experience. We were working on a major redesign of our product's dashboard. Instead of pushing it live to all users at once, we implemented a canary release. We started with 5% of our users, carefully selected to represent different user types and engagement levels.

Within the first hour, we noticed that load times for the new dashboard were significantly higher than expected for users with slower internet connections. Thanks to our canary release strategy, we were able to quickly roll back the change for that 5% and fix the issue before it affected our entire user base. Without the canary release, we might have faced a major outage and a lot of unhappy customers.

Diving into A/B Testing

What is A/B Testing?

Now that we've covered canary releases, let's talk about its close cousin: A/B testing. If canary releases are about cautiously rolling out new versions, A/B testing is about making data-driven decisions between different versions.

Imagine you're a chef developing a new recipe. Instead of just guessing which version your customers will prefer, you serve two slightly different versions and see which one gets better reviews. That's essentially what A/B testing is in the software world.

In A/B testing, you create two (or more) versions of a feature or page, show them to different groups of users, and then analyze which version performs better based on your predefined metrics.

Benefits of A/B Testing

1. **Data-Driven Decisions**: Instead of relying on gut feelings or assumptions, you're making decisions based on real user behavior and preferences.
2. **Continuous Improvement**: A/B testing allows you to constantly refine and improve your product, even in small increments.
3. **User Experience Optimization**: By testing different versions, you can identify what resonates best with your users, leading to a better overall user experience.
4. **Increased Conversions**: For businesses, A/B testing can lead to higher conversion rates by identifying the most effective designs or content.
5. **Risk Reduction**: Similar to canary releases, A/B testing allows you to test new ideas without committing to a full rollout.

Implementing A/B Testing

Here's how you can implement A/B testing in your development process:

1. **Identify Your Test Goal**: What are you trying to improve? It could be click-through rates, sign-ups, purchases, or any other measurable metric.
2. **Create Variations**: Develop two (or more) versions of the feature or page you want to test. These could be minor changes like button colors or major differences in layout or functionality.

3. **Split Your Audience**: Randomly divide your users into groups, each seeing a different version. Ensure your groups are large enough to provide statistically significant results.

4. **Run the Test**: Launch your variations and start collecting data. The duration of the test will depend on your specific circumstances, but it should be long enough to gather meaningful results.

5. **Analyze Results**: Once the test is complete, analyze the data to determine which version performed better according to your predefined metrics.

6. **Implement the Winner**: Roll out the winning version to all users and consider what you learned for future development.

A/B testing revealed that minor wording changes—like "Try It Free" versus "Start Free Trial"—can significantly impact user behavior, with one variation increasing click-through rates by 28%. This demonstrates how subtle linguistic differences can drive measurable performance improvements in conversion-focused elements.

Combining Canary Releases and A/B Testing

Now that we've explored canary releases and A/B testing separately, let's talk about how these two powerful techniques can work together to supercharge your deployment and testing strategy.

The Power of Combination

When you combine canary releases with A/B testing, you're creating a robust system for safely deploying new features while simultaneously gathering data on their effectiveness. Here's how it might work:

1. **Canary Release**: You start by releasing your new feature to a small percentage of your users (the canary group).

2. **A/B Test Within the Canary**: Within this canary group, you set up an A/B test, perhaps testing two slightly different versions of the new feature.

3. **Monitor and Analyze**: As the canary release progresses, you're not just monitoring for errors or performance issues, but also gathering data on which version of the feature is performing better.

4. **Gradual Rollout**: If the canary release is stable, you can gradually increase the percentage of users in the canary group, continuing the A/B test as you go.

5. **Full Deployment**: By the time you're ready for a full deployment, you not only know that the feature is stable, but you also have data on which version of the feature is most effective.

This combined approach gives you the best of both worlds: the safety and control of canary releases with the data-driven decision-making of A/B testing.

Real-World Example

Let me share a real-world example from a project I worked on. We were developing a new onboarding process for our SaaS product. We knew it was a critical part of the user experience, so we wanted to be extra careful with the rollout.

We started with a canary release to 10% of our new sign-ups. Within this group, we set up an A/B test:

- Version A: A step-by-step guided tour of the product
- Version B: A more hands-off approach with tooltips and a help button

We monitored closely for any technical issues while also tracking metrics like time to complete onboarding, feature adoption in the first week, and customer support tickets from new users.

After two weeks, we had some fascinating results. While both versions were technically stable, Version B was outperforming Version A in almost every metric. Users were completing onboarding faster, adopting more features, and generating fewer support tickets.

Based on this data, we gradually increased the canary group, continuing the A/B test. By the time we reached 50% of new sign-ups, the trend was clear. We then rolled out Version B to all new users, confident that we were providing the best possible onboarding experience.

This approach allowed us to:

1. Safely test a critical new feature
2. Make a data-driven decision between two design approaches
3. Gradually roll out the change, monitoring at each step
4. Significantly improve our onboarding process and, ultimately, user satisfaction

Metrics and Decision-Making for Full Rollout

One of the most critical aspects of both canary releases and A/B testing is knowing what to measure and how to make decisions based on those measurements. Let's dive into the metrics you should be tracking and how to use them to make informed decisions about your full rollout.

Key Metrics to Track

1. **Performance Metrics**
    - Response Time: How quickly does your application respond to user requests?
    - Error Rates: Are there any increases in errors or exceptions?
    - Resource Utilization: CPU, memory, disk I/O, network usage
2. **User Behavior Metrics**
    - Engagement: Time spent on site/app, number of pages viewed, features used
    - Conversion Rates: Signups, purchases, or any other key actions
    - Bounce Rates: Are users leaving faster than before?
3. **Business Metrics**
    - Revenue: Is the new version affecting your bottom line?
    - Customer Support Tickets: Are there more or fewer issues being reported?
    - User Satisfaction: Can be measured through surveys or Net Promoter Score (NPS)
4. **Technical Metrics**
    - Deployment Success Rate: Are there any issues during deployment?
    - Rollback Frequency: How often do you need to revert to the previous version?
    - Feature Flag Usage: Are the right users seeing the right features?

Collecting and Analyzing Data

Now that you know what to measure, how do you go about collecting and analyzing this data? Here are some approaches:

1. **Logging and Monitoring Tools**: Use tools like Prometheus, Grafana, or ELK stack to collect and visualize your performance and technical metrics.
2. **Analytics Platforms**: Tools like Google Analytics, Mixpanel, or Amplitude can help track user behavior metrics.

3. **A/B Testing Frameworks**: Platforms like Optimizely or Google Optimize can help manage your A/B tests and provide statistical analysis.
4. **Customer Feedback Tools**: Use surveys, in-app feedback mechanisms, or tools like UserVoice to gather qualitative data.
5. **Automated Alerts**: Set up alerting systems to notify you immediately if key metrics fall outside of acceptable ranges.

Remember, the goal is to have a holistic view of how your new version is performing. Don't focus too narrowly on any single metric.

Making the Decision to Fully Roll Out

So, you've gathered all this data. How do you decide when it's time for a full rollout? Here's a framework I've found helpful:

1. **Define Success Criteria in Advance**: Before you even start your canary release or A/B test, clearly define what success looks like. This might be "No increase in error rates, 5% improvement in conversion rate, and positive user feedback."
2. **Statistical Significance**: For A/B tests, ensure your results are statistically significant. Most A/B testing tools will calculate this for you.
3. **Trend Analysis**: Look at how metrics change over time. A positive initial response that declines might indicate novelty effect rather than true improvement.
4. **Segment Analysis**: Check if the results are consistent across different user segments. A feature that works well for power users but confuses new users might need refinement.
5. **Risk vs. Reward**: Balance the potential benefits of rolling out against the risks of issues you've identified.
6. **Stakeholder Input**: While data should drive the decision, input from stakeholders (product managers, customer support, etc.) can provide valuable context.
7. **Phased Rollout Plan**: Even when deciding to fully roll out, consider a phased approach, gradually increasing from your canary group to 100% of users.

Let me share a personal anecdote about making these decisions. We once had a feature that showed amazing improvements in our A/B test - conversion rates were up by 30%! The team was excited to roll it out fully. However, when we dug deeper into the data, we noticed that while conversions were up, the average order value had decreased, and customer support tickets for this group had increased slightly.

We decided to pause the full rollout and investigate further. It turned out that the new feature was indeed encouraging more purchases, but it was also causing some confusion that led to smaller orders and more support issues. We refined the feature, ran another test, and only then proceeded with a full rollout when we saw improvements across all our key metrics.

The lesson? Always look at the full picture. A win in one area might be masking issues in another.

Challenges and Best Practices

While canary releases and A/B testing are powerful tools, they come with their own set of challenges. Let's explore some common pitfalls and best practices to help you navigate these waters successfully.

Common Challenges

1. **Increased Complexity**: Managing multiple versions of your application simultaneously can be complex and resource-intensive.
2. **Data Volume and Analysis**: You'll be collecting a lot of data. Making sense of it all and drawing the right conclusions can be challenging.
3. **User Consistency**: Ensuring a consistent experience for users, especially in long-running tests, can be tricky.
4. **Performance Overhead**: Feature flags and A/B testing frameworks can introduce performance overhead if not implemented carefully.
5. **False Positives/Negatives**: Short-term results might not always translate to long-term success, leading to incorrect conclusions.
6. **Organizational Resistance**: Some team members or stakeholders might be resistant to this data-driven approach, preferring to rely on intuition or experience.

Best Practices

To address these challenges and get the most out of your canary releases and A/B tests, consider these best practices:

1. **Start Small and Scale**: Begin with simple tests and gradually increase complexity as your team gains experience.
2. **Invest in Infrastructure**: Good tooling for deployment, monitoring, and analysis is crucial. It's worth investing time and resources to get this right.

3. **Clear Documentation**: Maintain clear documentation of all tests, including hypotheses, parameters, and results. This helps with knowledge sharing and future decision-making.
4. **Cross-Functional Collaboration**: Involve different teams (development, ops, product, marketing) in the process. Each brings valuable perspectives.
5. **Consistent Evaluation Criteria**: Establish clear, consistent criteria for evaluating tests. This helps avoid bias and ensures fair comparisons between experiments.
6. **User Privacy and Consent**: Be transparent with users about testing and ensure you're complying with relevant data protection regulations.
7. **Limit Concurrent Tests**: Running too many tests simultaneously can lead to confusing results and interaction effects. Limit the number of concurrent experiments.
8. **Plan for Long-Term Effects**: While it's important to react to short-term data, also plan for measuring long-term effects of changes.
9. **Educate Stakeholders**: Help everyone in the organization understand the value of this approach. Share successes and learnings broadly.
10. **Continuous Improvement**: Regularly review and refine your testing processes. The way you approach canary releases and A/B testing should itself be subject to improvement and optimization.

Running excessive concurrent A/B tests creates overlapping variables that obscure data interpretation, making it difficult to isolate which changes actually impact user behavior. Proper test sequencing and controlled variables are essential for drawing actionable insights from experimentation.

We took a step back, simplified our approach, and focused on one or two key tests at a time. This not only made our analysis clearer but also allowed us to dedicate more resources to each test, resulting in more meaningful improvements.

Future Trends in Canary Releases and A/B Testing

As we wrap up our exploration of canary releases and A/B testing, let's look ahead to some emerging trends and future directions in this space. The world of software development is ever-evolving, and these techniques are no exception.

AI and Machine Learning Integration

Artificial Intelligence (AI) and Machine Learning (ML) are set to play an increasingly important role in canary releases and A/B testing:

1. **Automated Decision Making**: AI systems could analyze test results in real-time, making decisions about whether to continue, expand, or roll back a canary release without human intervention.
2. **Predictive Analytics**: ML models could predict the likely outcomes of A/B tests based on historical data, helping teams focus on the most promising experiments.
3. **Personalized Experiences**: AI could help create more sophisticated A/B tests that adapt to individual user preferences and behaviors.
4. **Anomaly Detection**: ML algorithms could more quickly and accurately detect anomalies during canary releases, improving safety and reliability.

Multivariate Testing and AI-Driven Experimentation

While A/B testing typically compares two variants, the future is likely to see more complex, multivariate tests:

1. **Multivariate Testing**: Instead of just A/B, we might see A/B/C/D testing or even more complex combinations.
2. **AI-Generated Variants**: AI systems could generate multiple variants of a feature to test, potentially discovering innovative solutions that humans might not have considered.
3. **Continuous Experimentation**: The line between development and experimentation may blur, with systems constantly testing and optimizing in real-time.

Integration with DevOps and CI/CD

Canary releases and A/B testing will likely become even more tightly integrated with DevOps practices and CI/CD pipelines:

1. **Automated Canary Analysis**: Tools that automatically analyze canary releases and make promotion/rollback decisions will become more sophisticated and widely adopted.
2. **Feature Flags as a Service**: More robust, scalable feature flag services will emerge, making it easier to manage complex rollout scenarios.

3. **Integrated Metrics and Observability**: Deeper integration between testing tools and observability platforms will provide more comprehensive insights into application and feature performance.

Ethical Considerations and Transparency

As these techniques become more powerful and pervasive, ethical considerations will come to the forefront:

1. **User Consent and Transparency**: There may be growing pressure or regulations requiring more explicit user consent and transparency about testing.
2. **Ethical AI in Testing**: As AI plays a larger role in testing, ensuring that these systems make ethical decisions will be crucial.
3. **Balancing Personalization and Privacy**: Finding the right balance between personalized experiences and user privacy will be an ongoing challenge.

Cross-Platform and Omnichannel Testing

As users interact with services across multiple platforms and channels, testing strategies will evolve:

1. **Cross-Platform Consistency**: Ensuring consistent experiences across web, mobile, and other platforms during testing will become increasingly important.
2. **Omnichannel Testing**: A/B tests may expand to cover user journeys that span multiple channels, from online to in-store experiences.

Democratization of Testing

Testing capabilities are likely to become more accessible to non-technical team members:

1. **No-Code Testing Tools**: We'll see more tools that allow product managers, marketers, and other non-developers to set up and run tests.
2. **Democratized Data Analysis**: Improved data visualization and analysis tools will make it easier for anyone in the organization to derive insights from test results.

As we look to the future, it's clear that canary releases and A/B testing will remain crucial tools in the software development toolkit. However, they will evolve to become more sophisticated, more integrated with other processes, and more accessible to a wider range of professionals.

The key for us as developers and project managers is to stay curious, keep learning, and be ready to adapt our practices as these new trends emerge. The fundamental principles we've discussed in this chapter – gradual rollouts, data-driven decision making, and continuous improvement – will remain relevant even as the specific tools and techniques evolve.

Remember, the goal is always to deliver better software, more safely, and with a deeper understanding of our users' needs and preferences. Canary releases and A/B testing, in whatever form they take in the future, will continue to be powerful allies in achieving that goal.

As we move on to the next chapter, keep in mind how these testing and deployment strategies fit into the broader context of software maintenance and support. The insights gained from canary releases and A/B tests will inform not just your initial deployments, but also your ongoing efforts to maintain and improve your software over time.

Chapter 17: Software Maintenance and Support

Introduction

Welcome to the often-overlooked but critically important world of software maintenance and support! If you're reading this, you've likely been through the exciting journey of developing and deploying software. But here's the thing - the work doesn't stop once your software goes live. In fact, for many projects, that's when the real challenge begins.

The completion of a major project often marks just the beginning, as maintenance, bug fixes, and feature requests quickly follow deployment. Software development extends beyond initial creation—it requires ongoing support and evolution to meet user needs.

In this chapter, we're going to dive deep into the world of software maintenance and support. We'll explore the different types of maintenance, discuss the importance of Service Level Agreements (SLAs), and look at effective strategies for incident management and resolution. By the end of this chapter, you'll have a comprehensive understanding of how to keep your software running smoothly long after the initial deployment.

Types of Maintenance

When we talk about software maintenance, we're not just talking about fixing bugs (although that's certainly part of it). There are actually several types of maintenance that you'll need to consider. Let's break them down:

Corrective Maintenance

This is probably what most people think of when they hear "software maintenance." Corrective maintenance involves fixing bugs and errors that were either not caught during testing or that have emerged after deployment.

I once worked on a project where we discovered a major security flaw a week after launch. We had to drop everything and work around the clock to patch it. That's corrective maintenance in action, and it's often the most urgent type of maintenance you'll deal with.

Here are some key aspects of corrective maintenance:

1. Bug tracking and prioritization
2. Root cause analysis
3. Quick turnaround times for critical issues
4. Thorough testing of fixes to avoid introducing new problems

Adaptive Maintenance

The tech world doesn't stand still, and neither should your software. Adaptive maintenance involves updating your software to work with new hardware, operating systems, or other external changes.

For example, when Apple introduced the notch on the iPhone X, many apps had to be updated to accommodate this new design feature. That's adaptive maintenance.

Key considerations for adaptive maintenance include:

1. Staying informed about upcoming changes in relevant technologies
2. Planning for updates well in advance
3. Ensuring backward compatibility where possible
4. Testing on new platforms or with new technologies

Perfective Maintenance

This type of maintenance is all about improving your software's performance and usability. It often involves adding new features or enhancing existing ones based on user feedback or changing business needs.

E-commerce platforms often undergo perfective maintenance through continuous feature additions driven by customer feedback, enhancing both utility and market competitiveness. This iterative improvement process keeps digital products aligned with evolving user needs and business goals.

When engaging in perfective maintenance, consider:

1. Gathering and analyzing user feedback

2. Prioritizing feature requests
3. Ensuring new features integrate smoothly with existing functionality
4. Performance testing to ensure improvements don't negatively impact system speed

Preventive Maintenance

As the saying goes, "An ounce of prevention is worth a pound of cure." Preventive maintenance involves updating your software to prevent future problems. This might include refactoring code to improve maintainability, updating libraries to patch known vulnerabilities, or optimizing database queries to prevent future performance issues.

In my experience, preventive maintenance is often the hardest to justify to stakeholders because it doesn't produce immediate, visible results. But it's crucial for the long-term health of your software.

Key aspects of preventive maintenance include:

1. Regular code reviews and refactoring
2. Keeping libraries and dependencies up to date
3. Performance optimization
4. Regular security audits

Service Level Agreements (SLAs)

Now that we've covered the types of maintenance, let's talk about an essential tool in managing maintenance and support: Service Level Agreements, or SLAs.

An SLA is a contract between you (the service provider) and your client that defines the level of service you're expected to provide. It sets clear expectations for both parties and can help prevent misunderstandings down the line.

Key Components of an SLA

A good SLA should include:

1. **Service Description**: What exactly are you providing? Be specific about what's included and what's not.
2. **Performance Metrics**: How will service quality be measured? This might include things like uptime, response time, or resolution time.
3. **Responsibilities**: What's expected from both the service provider and the client?

4. **Response Times**: How quickly will you respond to different types of issues?
5. **Resolution Times**: How quickly will different types of issues be resolved?
6. **Availability**: When will support be available? 24/7, business hours only, etc.
7. **Escalation Procedures**: What happens if an issue can't be resolved within the agreed-upon time?
8. **Penalties**: What happens if you fail to meet the agreed-upon service levels?

Creating Effective SLAs

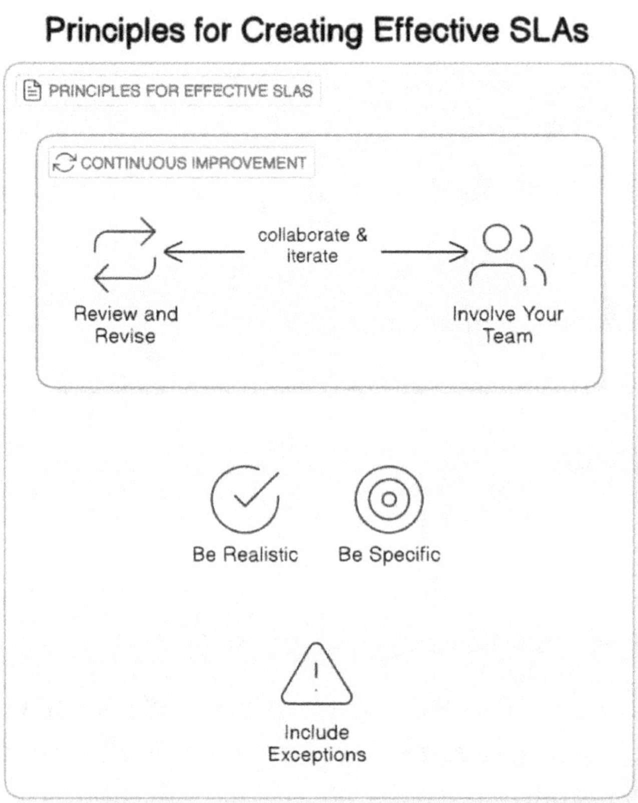

When creating an SLA, remember that it's not just a legal document - it's a tool for managing expectations and ensuring customer satisfaction. Here are some tips I've learned for creating effective SLAs:

1. **Be Realistic**: Don't promise what you can't deliver. It's better to under-promise and over-deliver than the other way around.
2. **Be Specific**: Vague language can lead to misunderstandings. Use clear, measurable terms.

3. **Include Exceptions**: There will always be circumstances beyond your control. Make sure your SLA accounts for these.

4. **Review and Revise**: An SLA shouldn't be set in stone. Review it regularly and adjust as needed based on real-world performance and changing needs.

5. **Involve Your Team**: The people who will be doing the actual support work should have input on what goes into the SLA.

Remember, an SLA is more than just a set of rules - it's a commitment to your clients. By setting clear expectations and consistently meeting them, you'll build trust and foster long-term relationships.

Incident Management and Resolution

Incident Management and Resolution Process

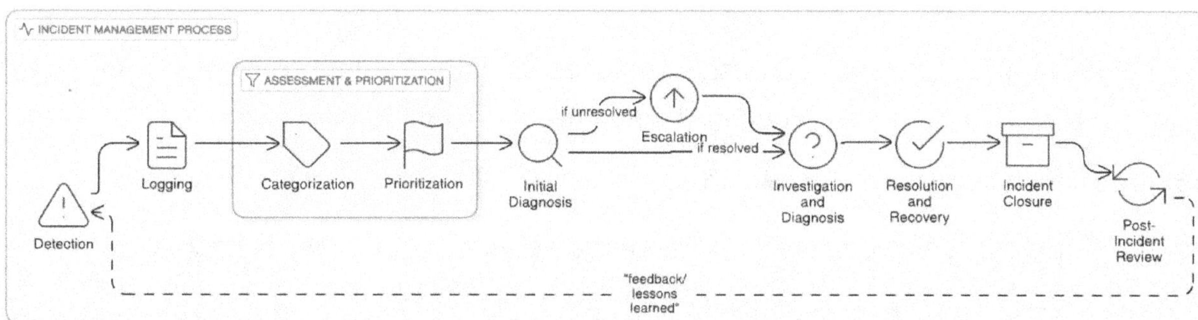

Even with the best preventive measures in place, incidents will occur. How you handle these incidents can make or break your relationship with your clients. Let's dive into some strategies for effective incident management and resolution.

The Incident Management Process

1. **Detection**: The first step is identifying that an incident has occurred. This could be through automated monitoring systems, user reports, or proactive checks by your team.

2. **Logging**: Once an incident is detected, it needs to be logged. This creates a record of the issue and starts the clock on your response time.

3. **Categorization**: Not all incidents are created equal. Categorize the incident based on its severity and impact. This helps in prioritizing your response.

4. **Prioritization**: Based on the categorization, determine how urgently the incident needs to be addressed. High-priority incidents that affect many users or critical functions should be tackled first.
5. **Initial Diagnosis**: Perform a quick assessment to understand the nature of the problem and its potential causes.
6. **Escalation**: If the incident can't be resolved by the initial responder, it needs to be escalated to the appropriate team or individual.
7. **Investigation and Diagnosis**: This is where you dig deep to find the root cause of the problem.
8. **Resolution and Recovery**: Implement the fix and restore normal service.
9. **Incident Closure**: Once the incident is resolved and normal service is restored, the incident can be closed.
10. **Post-Incident Review**: After the dust has settled, conduct a review to understand what happened, why it happened, and how to prevent similar incidents in the future.

Best Practices for Incident Resolution

Over the years, I've learned a few things about handling incidents effectively:

1. **Stay Calm**: Incidents can be stressful, but panicking never helps. Take a deep breath and approach the problem methodically.
2. **Communicate Clearly**: Keep stakeholders informed throughout the process. Be honest about what you know and what you don't know.
3. **Document Everything**: Detailed documentation of the incident and your response can be invaluable for future reference and for improving your processes.
4. **Learn from Each Incident**: Every incident is an opportunity to improve. Use what you learn to refine your processes and prevent future issues.
5. **Have a Plan**: Don't wait for an incident to occur to figure out how you'll handle it. Have clear procedures in place for different types of incidents.
6. **Use the Right Tools**: Invest in good incident management tools. They can help streamline your process and ensure nothing falls through the cracks.
7. **Practice**: Conduct regular drills to ensure your team is prepared to handle incidents effectively.

The Importance of Post-Incident Reviews

I can't stress enough how valuable post-incident reviews can be. They're not about pointing fingers or assigning blame - they're about learning and improving.

A good post-incident review should answer these questions:

1. What happened?
2. Why did it happen?
3. How did we respond?
4. What went well in our response?
5. What could we have done better?
6. How can we prevent similar incidents in the future?

These reviews can lead to improvements in your systems, your processes, and even your company culture. They're a key part of the continuous improvement cycle that's so crucial in software development and maintenance.

Balancing Maintenance and New Development

One of the biggest challenges in software maintenance is balancing the need to keep existing systems running smoothly with the pressure to develop new features or even entirely new products.

Organizations often struggle to balance new development and system maintenance—over-prioritizing innovation risks instability, while excessive maintenance stifles competitiveness. Finding the right equilibrium is crucial for sustainable technological growth.

Here are some strategies I've found effective for striking the right balance:

1. **Allocate Resources Wisely**: Dedicate a specific portion of your resources to maintenance and support. This could be a percentage of your team's time or a dedicated maintenance team.
2. **Plan for Maintenance**: Include maintenance tasks in your sprint planning or project roadmaps. Don't treat it as an afterthought.
3. **Automate Where Possible**: Use automated testing, monitoring, and deployment tools to reduce the manual effort required for maintenance tasks.

4. **Refactor Regularly**: Regular refactoring can make your code easier to maintain over time, reducing the overall maintenance burden.
5. **Educate Stakeholders**: Help your stakeholders understand the importance of maintenance. Sometimes, the best new feature you can add is making your existing features work better.
6. **Consider Maintenance in Design**: When developing new features, consider how they will be maintained. A feature that's difficult to maintain might not be worth implementing.
7. **Use Feature Flags**: Feature flags allow you to deploy new features gradually, making it easier to maintain stability while still innovating.

Remember, maintenance isn't just about keeping the lights on - it's about creating a stable foundation for future innovation.

The Human Side of Maintenance and Support

So far, we've talked a lot about processes and technologies, but there's another crucial aspect of maintenance and support that often gets overlooked: the human element.

The people providing maintenance and support are often the primary point of contact between your company and your users. They're not just fixing bugs - they're managing relationships, setting expectations, and representing your brand.

Here are some key considerations for the human side of maintenance and support:

Building a Strong Support Team

1. **Hire for Soft Skills**: Technical skills are important, but so are communication, empathy, and problem-solving abilities.
2. **Provide Ongoing Training**: Keep your team updated on new technologies and techniques, but also provide training in customer service and communication.
3. **Foster a Positive Culture**: Support work can be stressful. Create a culture where team members feel valued and supported.
4. **Encourage Knowledge Sharing**: Set up systems for your team to share knowledge and learn from each other's experiences.

Managing User Expectations

1. **Be Transparent**: If there's a problem, admit it. Users appreciate honesty.

2. **Set Realistic Timelines**: Don't promise what you can't deliver. It's better to exceed expectations than to fall short.
3. **Educate Users**: Sometimes, the best way to resolve an issue is to help users understand how to avoid it in the future.
4. **Listen to Feedback**: User feedback is invaluable for improving your product and your support processes.

Dealing with Difficult Situations

Even with the best processes in place, you'll sometimes face difficult situations. Maybe it's a critical bug that's causing significant problems for users, or a particularly upset customer. Here's how to handle these situations:

1. **Stay Professional**: No matter how heated the situation gets, maintain your composure.
2. **Empathize**: Try to see the situation from the user's perspective. Acknowledge their frustration.
3. **Focus on Solutions**: Instead of dwelling on the problem, focus on how you're going to fix it.
4. **Follow Up**: After resolving a difficult situation, follow up to ensure the user is satisfied with the resolution.

The Future of Software Maintenance and Support

As we wrap up this chapter, let's take a moment to look ahead. The field of software maintenance and support is constantly evolving, driven by changes in technology and user expectations.

Here are some trends I see shaping the future of maintenance and support:

1. **AI and Machine Learning**: These technologies are already being used to predict and prevent issues before they occur. I expect this trend to accelerate, with AI playing a bigger role in diagnosing and even resolving issues.
2. **Self-Service Options**: Users increasingly expect to be able to solve problems on their own. Advanced knowledge bases, chatbots, and other self-service tools will become more prevalent.

3. **Predictive Maintenance**: Just as in physical systems, predictive maintenance in software will become more common, using data analysis to identify potential issues before they cause problems.

4. **Continuous Deployment and Maintenance**: The line between development and maintenance will continue to blur, with updates and fixes being deployed more frequently and seamlessly.

5. **Remote Support Technologies**: With more systems moving to the cloud and more teams working remotely, technologies for providing remote support will continue to advance.

6. **Increased Focus on Security**: As cyber threats evolve, maintenance and support processes will need to place an even greater emphasis on security.

Conclusion

Software maintenance and support might not be the most glamorous part of software development, but it's absolutely crucial. It's what keeps your software running smoothly, your users happy, and your business growing.

Remember, maintenance isn't just about fixing what's broken - it's about continual improvement, adapting to change, and providing value to your users day after day, year after year.

As we move into the next chapter on performance monitoring and optimization, keep in mind that these activities are closely intertwined with maintenance and support. The insights you gain from monitoring your software's performance will inform your maintenance activities, and your maintenance work will directly impact your software's performance.

So, embrace the world of maintenance and support. It's challenging, it's important, and when done right, it can be incredibly rewarding. After all, there's nothing quite like the satisfaction of keeping a complex system running smoothly, knowing that your work is making a real difference for your users every single day.

Chapter 18: Performance Monitoring and Optimization

Introduction

Welcome to the exciting world of performance monitoring and optimization! As a seasoned software developer, I can't stress enough how crucial this aspect of the software development life cycle is. Think of your software as a finely tuned race car. Sure, it might look great and have all the latest features, but if it's not performing at its best, you're not going to win any races. That's where performance monitoring and optimization come in.

In this chapter, we're going to dive deep into the tools, techniques, and strategies that will help you keep your software running smoothly and efficiently. Whether you're dealing with a small application or a large-scale enterprise system, the principles we'll discuss here will be invaluable in ensuring your software performs at its peak.

The Importance of Performance Monitoring and Optimization

Before we get into the nitty-gritty, let's talk about why this topic is so important. I remember working on a project early in my career where we built this fantastic e-commerce platform. It looked great, had all the features the client wanted, and we were pretty proud of ourselves. Then came launch day. Within hours, the site was crawling, customers were complaining, and our client was... well, let's just say they weren't happy.

That experience taught me a valuable lesson: performance isn't just a nice-to-have, it's essential. Poor performance can lead to:

1. Lost revenue
2. Damaged reputation
3. Increased operational costs
4. Poor user experience
5. Decreased productivity

On the flip side, when you get performance right, you're looking at happier users, lower costs, and a competitive edge in the market. So, let's roll up our sleeves and get into it!

Monitoring Tools and Techniques

Application Performance Monitoring (APM) Tools

When it comes to monitoring your application's performance, you're not flying blind. There's a whole suite of tools designed to give you insights into how your software is performing. These are called Application Performance Monitoring (APM) tools, and they're your best friends in the world of performance optimization.

Some popular APM tools include:

1. New Relic
2. Datadog

3. Dynatrace
4. AppDynamics
5. Nagios

These tools provide real-time insights into your application's performance, helping you identify bottlenecks, track user experiences, and pinpoint issues before they become major problems.

Application performance monitoring tools like New Relic can quickly detect anomalies—such as sudden API response time spikes—and pinpoint root causes like inefficient database queries. Proactive monitoring enables teams to resolve performance issues before they impact users.

Key Performance Indicators (KPIs)

When you're monitoring performance, you need to know what to look for. That's where Key Performance Indicators (KPIs) come in. These are the metrics that matter most for your application's performance. Some common KPIs include:

1. Response Time: How long does it take for your application to respond to a request?
2. Throughput: How many requests can your application handle per unit of time?
3. Error Rate: What percentage of requests result in errors?
4. CPU Usage: How much of your server's processing power is being used?
5. Memory Usage: How much RAM is your application consuming?
6. Database Performance: How long do database queries take to execute?

Remember, the specific KPIs that matter most will depend on your application. For a high-traffic e-commerce site, throughput and response time might be critical. For a data-intensive analytics application, CPU and memory usage might be more important.

Real User Monitoring (RUM)

While server-side metrics are important, they don't tell the whole story. That's where Real User Monitoring (RUM) comes in. RUM tools collect data from actual users' browsers or devices, giving you insights into the real-world performance of your application.

RUM can help you understand:

1. Page load times

2. Network latency
3. Browser rendering times
4. User interactions and journeys

Server-side metrics alone can miss critical frontend performance issues—like third-party JavaScript delays—that directly impact user experience. Real User Monitoring (RUM) reveals these browser-side bottlenecks that traditional server metrics overlook, highlighting the importance of full-stack performance visibility!

Synthetic Monitoring

While RUM gives you data from real users, synthetic monitoring allows you to proactively test your application's performance. With synthetic monitoring, you create scripts that simulate user interactions with your application. These scripts can be run at regular intervals from various locations around the world.

Synthetic monitoring is great for:

1. Checking availability and uptime
2. Testing critical user journeys
3. Benchmarking performance over time
4. Identifying geographic-specific issues

I've found synthetic monitoring particularly useful for catching issues before they affect real users. For instance, on one project, our synthetic tests alerted us to a performance degradation in our European data center. We were able to address the issue before our European users started their workday.

Performance Tuning Strategies

Now that we've covered monitoring, let's talk about what to do when you identify performance issues. Performance tuning is part science, part art, and a whole lot of detective work. Here are some strategies I've found effective over the years:

1. Database Optimization

In my experience, database performance is often the bottleneck in web applications. Here are some techniques for optimizing database performance:

- Indexing: Properly indexed tables can dramatically speed up query execution times.

- Query Optimization: Rewriting inefficient queries can yield significant performance improvements.
- Denormalization: In some cases, strategic denormalization can speed up read operations.
- Caching: Implementing a caching layer can reduce database load for frequently accessed data.

Poorly optimized database queries can cripple performance—like a 10-second product search—but proper indexing and tuning can reduce response times by 100x or more. Database optimization remains one of the most impactful ways to improve application performance.

2. Code Profiling

Sometimes, performance issues lie in your application code. Code profiling tools can help you identify which parts of your code are taking the most time to execute. Some popular profiling tools include:

- Visual Studio Profiler for .NET applications
- JProfiler for Java applications
- XDebug for PHP applications

Once you've identified the slow parts of your code, you can optimize them. This might involve:

- Algorithmic improvements
- Caching results of expensive operations
- Removing unnecessary computations

Performance profiling often reveals unexpected bottlenecks—like a single function consuming 50% of CPU time—that can be optimized through techniques such as caching. Targeted optimizations based on profiling data can dramatically improve overall application efficiency.

3. Front-End Optimization

Don't forget about the front-end! A slow-loading front-end can make your application feel sluggish even if your back-end is lightning fast. Some front-end optimization techniques include:

- Minifying and compressing assets (CSS, JavaScript, images)
- Implementing lazy loading for images and other resources
- Using Content Delivery Networks (CDNs) for static assets
- Optimizing the critical rendering path

Basic optimizations like enabling Gzip compression and leveraging CDNs for static assets can dramatically improve performance—potentially halving page load times. These straightforward techniques often deliver disproportionate improvements for minimal implementation effort.

4. Caching Strategies

Caching is a powerful tool in your performance optimization toolkit. By storing frequently accessed data in memory, you can significantly reduce the load on your database and speed up response times. Some caching strategies to consider:

- In-memory caching (e.g., Redis, Memcached)
- HTTP caching
- Content Delivery Network (CDN) caching
- Application-level caching

Remember, caching isn't a silver bullet. It comes with its own challenges, like cache invalidation and maintaining consistency. As the old saying goes, "There are only two hard things in Computer Science: cache invalidation and naming things."

5. Asynchronous Processing

For operations that don't need to happen in real-time, consider moving them to asynchronous background processes. This can help improve response times for your users. Some examples of operations that can often be done asynchronously:

- Sending emails
- Generating reports
- Processing large datasets
- Updating search indexes

Moving non-critical operations—such as email confirmations and inventory updates—to background jobs can transform user experience, reducing order processing from seconds to near-instant responses. This architectural approach prioritizes perceived performance while maintaining all necessary business logic.

6. Horizontal Scaling

Sometimes, the best way to improve performance is simply to throw more resources at the problem. Horizontal scaling involves adding more machines to your resource pool. This is in contrast to vertical scaling, which involves adding more power (CPU, RAM) to an existing machine.

Horizontal scaling can be particularly effective for handling increased load. However, it requires your application to be designed in a way that can take advantage of distributed resources. This often involves:

- Stateless application design
- Distributed caching
- Load balancing

I've worked on systems where we were able to handle a 10x increase in traffic simply by spinning up more application servers behind a load balancer. Of course, this approach has its limits - at some point, you'll need to optimize your application to truly scale.

Capacity Planning and Scaling

Performance optimization isn't just about making your current system run faster - it's also about planning for the future. Capacity planning is the process of determining the resources you'll need to meet future demand.

Understanding Your Current Capacity

The first step in capacity planning is understanding your current capacity. This involves:

1. Identifying your current peak load
2. Understanding your resource utilization during peak times
3. Identifying any current bottlenecks

Your monitoring tools will be invaluable here. Look at historical data to understand patterns in your resource usage.

Forecasting Future Demand

Once you understand your current capacity, you need to forecast future demand. This might involve:

1. Analyzing historical growth trends
2. Considering upcoming features or marketing initiatives that might drive increased usage
3. Planning for seasonal variations in traffic

E-commerce platforms must prepare for peak traffic events like Black Friday—relying on average load estimates risks catastrophic outages during critical sales periods. Proactive capacity planning is essential to maintain availability when it matters most!

Scaling Strategies

When it comes to scaling, you have two main options: vertical scaling and horizontal scaling.

Vertical Scaling

Vertical scaling, also known as "scaling up," involves adding more power to your existing machines. This might mean upgrading to a more powerful CPU, adding more RAM, or using faster storage.

Pros of vertical scaling:

- Simple to implement
- Can be effective for smaller applications

Cons of vertical scaling:

- There's a limit to how much you can scale vertically
- Can be expensive
- Often requires downtime to implement

Horizontal Scaling

Horizontal scaling, or "scaling out," involves adding more machines to your resource pool. This is often the preferred approach for large-scale applications.

Pros of horizontal scaling:

- Can scale to meet almost any level of demand
- Can be more cost-effective than vertical scaling
- Can improve fault tolerance

Cons of horizontal scaling:

- Requires applications to be designed for distributed computing
- Can increase complexity of your system

In my experience, most modern applications end up using a combination of both vertical and horizontal scaling. You might vertically scale your database server while horizontally scaling your application servers, for instance.

Auto-Scaling

For applications with variable load, auto-scaling can be a game-changer. Auto-scaling automatically adjusts the number of servers based on current demand. This can help you handle traffic spikes without paying for unused capacity during quiet periods.

Auto-scaling in cloud platforms like AWS and Azure efficiently handles fluctuating demand—automatically expanding resources during predictable traffic surges (like exam periods) and reducing them during lulls (like holidays). This ensures optimal performance while controlling costs.

Continuous Performance Testing

Performance optimization isn't a one-time task - it's an ongoing process. As your application evolves and your user base grows, new performance challenges will emerge. That's why it's crucial to implement continuous performance testing.

Integrating Performance Tests into Your CI/CD Pipeline

By integrating performance tests into your Continuous Integration/Continuous Deployment (CI/CD) pipeline, you can catch performance regressions before they make it to production. Some strategies for this include:

1. Running load tests on every build
2. Setting performance budgets and failing builds that exceed them
3. Comparing performance metrics between builds

Continuous integration performance tests can catch critical regressions—like accidental algorithmic complexity changes from O(n) to $O(n^2)$—preventing production incidents. Automated performance validation in CI/CD pipelines serves as an essential safety net for code quality.

A/B Testing for Performance

A/B testing isn't just for user interface changes - it can also be a powerful tool for performance optimization. By releasing performance improvements to a subset of your users, you can:

1. Validate the impact of your optimizations
2. Identify any unexpected side effects
3. Gradually roll out changes to minimize risk

Performance testing in staging environments provides real-world validation for optimizations—whether evaluating new caching layers or major architectural shifts—before production deployment. This controlled proving ground helps confirm improvements while minimizing user impact.

Conclusion

Performance monitoring and optimization is a vast and complex field, but I hope this chapter has given you a solid foundation to build upon. Remember, the key to successful performance optimization is a data-driven approach. Use your monitoring tools to identify issues, measure the impact of your optimizations, and continuously iterate.

As we wrap up, let me leave you with one final piece of advice: always optimize with your users in mind. It's easy to get caught up in technical metrics, but at the end of the day, what matters most is the experience of the people using your software. A millisecond improvement in server response time might look great on paper, but if it doesn't translate to a noticeable improvement for your users, it might not be worth the effort.

In the next chapter, we'll be discussing software updates and patch management - another critical aspect of maintaining a healthy, performant software system. Until then, happy optimizing!

Chapter 19: Software Updates and Patch Management

Introduction

Welcome to the world of software updates and patch management! If you've ever used a computer or smartphone, you've undoubtedly encountered the familiar prompt: "A new update is available. Would you like to install it now?" As a software developer or IT professional, you're on the other side of this process, responsible for creating, testing, and distributing these updates. In this chapter, we'll dive deep into the strategies and best practices that make this crucial aspect of software maintenance run smoothly.

Deploying significant software updates carries inherent risks like data loss or regression bugs, making structured version control, patch management, and distribution protocols essential. Proper implementation of these safeguards ensures updates enhance rather than disrupt user experience.

Versioning Strategies

Let's start with the foundation of any good update system: versioning. You might think, "It's just a number, right? How complicated can it be?" Oh, my friend, you'd be surprised! A solid versioning strategy is like a good map – it tells you where you've been, where you are, and where you're going.

Semantic Versioning

One of the most popular versioning strategies is Semantic Versioning (SemVer). It's a simple set of rules that dictates how version numbers are assigned and incremented. Here's how it works:

Given a version number MAJOR.MINOR.PATCH, increment the:

1. MAJOR version when you make incompatible API changes,
2. MINOR version when you add functionality in a backwards-compatible manner, and
3. PATCH version when you make backwards-compatible bug fixes.

For example, version 2.3.1 would indicate the second major release, with three minor releases and one patch.

Neglecting strict versioning conventions like SemVer leads to update chaos—unpredictable changes and confused users. Adhering to a clear versioning strategy prevents these issues by maintaining transparent, standardized release communication!

Calendar Versioning

Another approach is Calendar Versioning (CalVer). This strategy uses a date-based version number, often in the format YEAR.MONTH.PATCH. For instance, Ubuntu Linux uses this system – version 20.04 was released in April 2020.

CalVer can be particularly useful for projects with regular, time-based releases. It immediately communicates to users how recent a version is, which can be valuable information.

Choosing the Right Strategy

So, which strategy should you choose? It depends on your project and your users. If you're developing a library or API that other developers will use, SemVer might be the way to go. It clearly communicates when breaking changes occur. If you're working on an application with frequent updates, CalVer could be more appropriate.

Remember, the goal is clarity. Whatever system you choose, make sure it's consistent and well-documented.

Patch Development and Testing

Now that we've got our versioning sorted, let's talk about actually developing and testing these patches. This is where the rubber meets the road – or in our case, where the code meets the compiler.

Identifying Issues

The first step in patch development is identifying what needs to be fixed or improved. This could come from various sources:

- Bug reports from users
- Internal testing and QA processes
- Security vulnerabilities discovered by your team or external researchers
- New feature requests

Relying exclusively on user-reported issues often leads to missed optimization opportunities, as many problems go unreported. Proactive issue identification through systematic monitoring and analysis is essential for comprehensive system improvement.

Prioritizing Patches

Once you've identified potential issues, you need to prioritize them. Not all patches are created equal. Consider factors like:

- Severity of the issue (Is it a minor annoyance or a critical security flaw?)
- Number of users affected
- Complexity of the fix
- Potential impact on other parts of the system

A prioritization matrix can be helpful here. Plot your issues on a grid with "Impact" on one axis and "Effort" on the other. This visual representation can help you quickly identify which issues to tackle first.

Developing the Patch

When it comes to actually writing the patch, follow these best practices:

1. **Isolate the change**: Make sure your patch addresses only the specific issue at hand. Resist the temptation to refactor unrelated code or add new features.
2. **Write tests**: Before you even start coding the fix, write tests that demonstrate the issue. Then, write tests that will pass when the issue is resolved.
3. **Document the change**: Clear documentation is crucial. Explain what the patch does, why it's necessary, and any potential side effects.
4. **Review the code**: Even if you're working solo, take a step back and review your own code. Better yet, have a colleague review it if possible.

Rigorous Testing

Once the patch is developed, it's time for thorough testing. This isn't just about making sure the specific issue is fixed – you need to ensure the patch doesn't introduce new problems.

1. **Unit Testing**: Start with unit tests to verify that individual components are working correctly.
2. **Integration Testing**: Ensure that the patched component still works correctly with other parts of the system.
3. **Regression Testing**: Run your full suite of tests to catch any unintended consequences.
4. **Performance Testing**: Verify that the patch doesn't negatively impact system performance.
5. **Security Testing**: If applicable, conduct security tests to ensure the patch doesn't introduce new vulnerabilities.

When critical bug fixes deploy without sufficient testing, they frequently create cascading failures that require emergency rollbacks—damaging credibility. Implementing layered testing strategies (unit, integration, regression) forms an essential safety net for all updates!

Distribution and Installation Processes

Great! You've developed and tested your patch. Now comes the challenge of getting it into your users' hands. This process can vary widely depending on your software and user base, but let's cover some common approaches and best practices.

Update Channels

Consider implementing multiple update channels. This allows you to control the rollout of your patches and gives users more control over when they receive updates. Common channels include:

1. **Stable**: For most users, this channel receives well-tested updates that are considered safe for general use.
2. **Beta**: For users who want early access to new features and are willing to accept some instability.
3. **Nightly**: For developers and power users who want the absolute latest changes, bugs and all.

By using multiple channels, you can catch potential issues before they reach your entire user base. I've found this especially useful for catching compatibility issues that might not show up in your testing environment.

Automatic vs. Manual Updates

Decide whether your updates will be automatic or manual (or offer both options). There are pros and cons to each approach:

Automatic Updates:

- Pros: Ensures users are always on the latest version, can quickly patch security vulnerabilities.
- Cons: Can be disruptive, may cause issues if users are in the middle of important work.

Manual Updates:

- Pros: Gives users control over when to update, allows them to prepare for potential changes.
- Cons: Users may delay important updates, leading to fragmentation of your user base.

In my experience, a hybrid approach often works best. Critical security patches can be automatic, while larger feature updates are manual.

Incremental Updates

For large software packages, consider implementing incremental updates. Instead of downloading the entire software package for each update, only the changed components are downloaded. This can significantly reduce download times and bandwidth usage, especially for users with slower internet connections.

Update Notifications

How you communicate updates to your users is crucial. Clear, informative update notifications can improve user experience and increase update adoption rates. Include:

- What's new or fixed in the update
- The size of the update
- Estimated installation time
- Any actions required from the user

How Clear Update Notifications Improve Adoption Rates

Vague or overly technical update notifications often lead to hesitation or disengagement from users. By shifting to clear, user-friendly messaging, teams can significantly increase update adoption. Here's how to optimize notifications:

Key Principles for Effective Update Communication

1. **Prioritize Clarity Over Jargon**
    - Replace technical terms (e.g., "patched vulnerabilities") with outcome-focused language (e.g., "This update strengthens your account security").
    - Example:
        - *Unclear:* "Optimized API response handling."
        - *User-friendly:* "Faster load times for your dashboard."
2. **Emphasize User Benefits**
    - Answer the question: *Why should users care?* Highlight tangible improvements like speed, security, or new features.
3. **Build Trust with Transparency**

   - For critical updates, briefly explain the importance without overwhelming details:
      - "This includes essential security fixes—install now to stay protected."

4. **Design for Scannability**
   - Use bullet points, headers, or bold text to make updates easy to skim.
   - Optional: Add emojis or icons sparingly to draw attention to key points.

Advanced Strategies

- **Segment Your Audience:** Offer a "Technical Details" toggle for advanced users while keeping the default message simple.
- **Bundle Frequent Updates:** Summarize changes monthly/quarterly to avoid notification fatigue.

Clear communication bridges the gap between product improvements and user action—applying these principles can boost engagement not just for updates, but across UX writing, marketing, and beyond.

Rollback Capability

Always provide a way to roll back updates. No matter how thorough your testing, there's always a chance something could go wrong in the wild. A rollback feature can be a lifesaver in these situations.

Distribution Infrastructure

Ensure your distribution infrastructure can handle the load. If you're pushing out an update to millions of users simultaneously, you need robust servers and content delivery networks (CDNs) to manage the traffic.

Installation Process

Make the installation process as smooth as possible. This might include:

1. **Background Downloads**: Download updates in the background to minimize disruption.
2. **Scheduled Installations**: Allow users to schedule updates for convenient times.
3. **Progress Indicators**: Provide clear progress indicators during the update process.

4. **Error Handling**: Implement robust error handling and provide clear messages if something goes wrong.

Post-Update Procedures

Your job isn't done once the update is installed. Implement post-update procedures to ensure everything is working as expected.

Verification

After installation, your software should verify that the update was applied correctly. This might involve checking file integrity, updating database schemas, or running a suite of tests.

Telemetry

Consider implementing telemetry to gather data on update success rates and any issues that occur. This can help you quickly identify and address problems. Of course, be transparent with users about what data you're collecting and why.

User Feedback

Provide an easy way for users to give feedback on the update. This could be as simple as a "How's the new version working for you?" prompt, or a more detailed feedback form.

Monitoring

Closely monitor support channels and error logs immediately after pushing an update. This is often when critical issues will surface.

Conclusion

Whew! We've covered a lot of ground in this chapter. From version strategies to patch development, testing, and distribution, you now have a comprehensive understanding of software updates and patch management.

Remember, the goal of all this effort is to provide a better experience for your users. Every update is an opportunity to improve your software, fix issues, and delight your users. With the strategies and best practices we've discussed, you're well-equipped to turn the often-dreaded "update available" notification into something your users look forward to.

As we move into the next chapter on performance monitoring and optimization, keep in mind how the update process we've discussed here plays a crucial role in continuously improving your software's performance. The ability to quickly develop, test, and distribute patches is a key component of maintaining high-performing, user-friendly software in today's fast-paced tech landscape

Chapter 20: Legacy System Modernization

Introduction

Welcome to the world of legacy system modernization! If you're reading this chapter, chances are you're facing the daunting task of updating an outdated system that's been the backbone of your organization for years, maybe even decades. Don't worry; you're not alone. I've been there, and I'm here to guide you through this challenging but rewarding process.

Many organizations still rely on aging mainframe systems—some dating back to the 1980s—to power core operations like banking, logistics, or data processing. While these systems are often stable, they come with significant drawbacks:

- **High maintenance costs**
- **Limited flexibility** for upgrades or integrations
- **Compatibility challenges** with modern applications

These pain points make **legacy system modernization** a critical priority in today's software development lifecycle. Whether it's migrating to cloud-native architectures, adopting microservices, or refactoring monolithic codebases, updating outdated infrastructure is no longer optional for businesses competing in a fast-moving digital landscape.

In this chapter, we're going to dive deep into the world of legacy systems. We'll explore how to assess these systems, discuss various modernization strategies, and look at phased migration approaches. By the end of this chapter, you'll have a solid understanding of how to breathe new life into your aging systems, ensuring they can keep up with the demands of today's fast-paced digital world.

Assessing Legacy Systems

Before we can modernize a legacy system, we need to understand what we're dealing with. This assessment phase is crucial, and it's where I always start with my clients. Let's break it down into manageable steps.

Defining Legacy Systems

First things first: what exactly is a legacy system? In my experience, it's any system that meets one or more of these criteria:

1. It's outdated technologically
2. It's difficult or expensive to maintain

3. It lacks support from the vendor
4. It doesn't meet current business needs effectively

Now, it's important to note that age alone doesn't make a system "legacy." I've seen 5-year-old systems that were more problematic than some 20-year-old workhorses. It's all about how well the system meets current needs and how easily it can be maintained and updated.

Conducting a System Audit

Once we've identified our legacy systems, it's time for a thorough audit. Here's how I typically approach this:

1. **Functionality Assessment**: What does the system do? How well does it perform its intended functions? Are there any gaps between what it does and what the business needs?
2. **Technical Assessment**: What technologies does it use? Are they still supported? How difficult is it to find developers who can work with these technologies?
3. **Integration Capabilities**: How well does the system integrate with other systems? Can it easily connect to modern APIs and services?
4. **Performance Evaluation**: How does the system perform under current workloads? Are there performance bottlenecks?
5. **Security Analysis**: Does the system meet current security standards? Are there vulnerabilities that can't be easily addressed?
6. **Maintenance Costs**: How much time and money is spent maintaining the system? Is this cost increasing over time?
7. **Business Value**: How critical is this system to current business operations? What would be the impact if it failed?

Identifying Pain Points

During the assessment, you'll likely uncover several pain points. These are the issues that are causing the most frustration for users, developers, and the business as a whole. In my experience, common pain points include:

- Slow performance
- Inability to integrate with modern systems
- High maintenance costs

- Lack of features needed for current business processes
- Security vulnerabilities
- Difficulty in making changes or updates

Slow, legacy inventory management systems can create bottlenecks across the entire supply chain—leading to delays, inefficiencies, and direct financial losses. For retail businesses, these operational hurdles often translate into missed sales opportunities, excess stock, and frustrated customers.

Modernizing such systems isn't just about technology upgrades; it's a strategic move to protect revenue, improve agility, and stay competitive in fast-moving markets.

Gathering Stakeholder Input

Don't forget to talk to the people who use the system day in and day out. They often have invaluable insights into what's working, what's not, and what improvements would make the biggest difference. I always make sure to interview a range of stakeholders, from C-level executives to front-line employees.

Documenting the Current State

Finally, pull all of this information together into a comprehensive document that outlines the current state of your legacy system. This will be your roadmap as you move forward with modernization efforts.

Modernization Strategies

Now that we've assessed our legacy system, it's time to look at our options for modernization. There's no one-size-fits-all solution here; the best approach will depend on your specific situation. Let's explore some of the most common strategies.

Rehosting (Lift and Shift)

Rehosting, often called "lift and shift," is the simplest modernization strategy. It involves moving the legacy system from its current environment (often on-premises) to a new environment (typically the cloud) with minimal changes to the code.

Pros:

- Quick and relatively low-risk
- Minimal disruption to business operations
- Can provide immediate benefits in terms of infrastructure cost savings

Cons:

- Doesn't address underlying issues with the legacy code
- May not take full advantage of cloud capabilities

For organizations facing high data center costs, migrating legacy systems (like ERP platforms) to the cloud can deliver immediate cost relief. This approach not only reduces infrastructure expenses but also creates flexibility for a more phased, strategic modernization roadmap.

By prioritizing quick wins—such as cloud adoption—teams can free up budget and time to plan long-term transformations without disrupting critical operations.

Refactoring

Refactoring involves restructuring and optimizing the existing code without changing its external behavior. This can involve breaking monolithic applications into microservices, improving the code structure, or updating to more modern coding practices.

Pros:

- Improves code quality and maintainability
- Can be done incrementally, reducing risk
- Preserves existing functionality while improving the underlying structure

Cons:

- Can be time-consuming and complex
- Requires deep understanding of the existing codebase
- May not address all limitations of the legacy system

Refactoring proves highly effective for systems with solid architectural foundations that have accumulated technical debt over time. When codebases become brittle due to years of incremental patches and short-term fixes, targeted refactoring can restore maintainability without requiring full-scale redevelopment.

This approach preserves core functionality while addressing the accumulated complexities that hinder system evolution and developer productivity.

Rearchitecting

Rearchitecting is a more comprehensive approach that involves redesigning the application from the ground up. This might involve moving to a completely new architecture, such as shifting from a monolithic to a microservices architecture.

Pros:

- Allows for a complete redesign to meet current and future needs
- Can take full advantage of modern technologies and cloud-native capabilities
- Opportunity to significantly improve performance, scalability, and maintainability

Cons:

- High risk and potentially high cost
- Can be time-consuming
- May require significant retraining for developers and users

Many healthcare providers face limitations with monolithic patient management systems that struggle to adapt to evolving needs. Transitioning to a microservices architecture can deliver significant improvements, including:

- **Enhanced agility** for faster feature development
- **Improved interoperability** with other healthcare systems
- **Scalable infrastructure** to accommodate growing demands

This architectural shift addresses critical challenges in digital healthcare transformation while maintaining system reliability and patient data security..

Replacing (Rebuild)

Sometimes, the best option is to completely replace the legacy system with a new, custom-built solution or an off-the-shelf product.

Pros:

- Allows for a fresh start with modern technologies
- Can be tailored to exactly meet current business needs
- Opportunity to reimagine processes and workflows

Cons:

- Highest risk and potentially highest cost
- Can be disruptive to business operations during transition
- May require significant change management efforts

Replacing a system is a big decision, but sometimes it's necessary. I worked with a manufacturing company that replaced their 30-year-old custom inventory system with a modern ERP system. It was a challenging transition, but ultimately transformed their operations.

Retiring

Don't forget that sometimes the best modernization strategy is to retire the system altogether. If a legacy system is no longer providing value and its functions can be absorbed by other systems or are no longer needed, retirement should be considered.

Pros:

- Eliminates maintenance costs and complexity
- Can simplify the overall IT landscape

Cons:

- May require careful planning to ensure no critical functions are lost
- Could face resistance from users who are accustomed to the old system

Organizations often maintain outdated reporting systems long after modern BI tools have made them redundant. Proactively retiring such legacy systems can deliver immediate benefits:

- **Cost reduction** from eliminating maintenance and licensing fees
- **Simplified architecture** by removing redundant systems
- **Improved efficiency** through consolidated analytics workflows

This type of technology rationalization represents a strategic opportunity to reduce technical debt while capitalizing on modern data capabilities.

Phased Migration Approaches

Once you've chosen your modernization strategy, it's time to think about implementation. In most cases, a phased approach is the way to go. It reduces risk, allows for incremental improvements, and can help manage the impact on business operations. Let's look at some effective phased migration approaches.

Strangler Fig Pattern

The Strangler Fig Pattern, named after a type of vine that slowly "strangles" its host tree, is a gradual approach to replacing a legacy system. The idea is to build a new system around the edges of the old one, slowly replacing functionality until the old system is "strangled" and can be decommissioned.

Here's how it typically works:

1. Identify a piece of functionality in the legacy system that can be replaced.
2. Build a new component to handle this functionality.
3. Redirect traffic for this functionality from the old system to the new component.
4. Repeat this process, gradually replacing more and more of the legacy system.

A proven strategy for modernizing monolithic e-commerce systems involves phased component replacement, beginning with discrete functional modules like:

1. **Product catalog** (typically the easiest to decouple)
2. **Shopping cart functionality**
3. **Order processing systems**

This incremental approach delivers several advantages:

- **Minimizes business disruption** by avoiding "big bang" migrations
- **Provides measurable milestones** to demonstrate ROI throughout the process
- **Reduces risk** through gradual validation of each new component

While requiring more time than a full rewrite, this method ensures continuity while systematically replacing technical debt with modern architecture.

Pros:

- Reduces risk by allowing for incremental changes
- Provides value early and often
- Allows for course correction along the way

Cons:

- Can take longer than a "big bang" approach
- Requires careful management of the transition period when both old and new systems are running

Parallel Run

In a parallel run approach, you build the new system alongside the old one, and run both systems simultaneously for a period of time. This allows you to verify that the new system is working correctly before fully decommissioning the old one.

Here's a typical process:

1. Build the new system while keeping the old one running.
2. Migrate a subset of data and users to the new system.
3. Run both systems in parallel, comparing outputs to ensure accuracy.
4. Gradually migrate more data and users to the new system.
5. Once confident in the new system, decommission the old one.

For mission-critical systems where precision is non-negotiable – particularly in regulated industries like financial services – running legacy and modernized systems in parallel provides essential verification. The financial sector often employs this approach with:

Key Implementation Parameters:

- **Full quarter comparison period** (aligns with standard financial reporting cycles)
- **Exact output matching** across all reports before cutover
- **Gradual transition** only after complete validation

Strategic Benefits:

- **Risk mitigation** through empirical verification
- **Regulatory compliance** assurance
- **Zero-tolerance accuracy** for financial data integrity

This methodology proves particularly valuable for financial reporting systems, core banking platforms, and other systems where even minor discrepancies could have significant consequences.

Pros:

- Provides a safety net during the transition
- Allows for thorough testing and validation
- Can help build confidence in the new system

Cons:

- Requires maintaining two systems simultaneously, which can be resource-intensive
- Can be confusing for users who need to work with both systems
- May require data synchronization between the old and new systems

Incremental Data Migration

When dealing with large, complex databases, an incremental data migration approach can be very effective. Instead of trying to migrate all data at once, you move it in stages.

Here's how it might look:

1. Start by migrating static or reference data.
2. Move historical data that doesn't change frequently.
3. Set up real-time synchronization for active data.
4. Gradually shift write operations to the new system.
5. Once all data is migrated and in sync, cut over completely to the new system.

A structured, three-phase methodology proves effective for modernizing telecom customer databases while maintaining operational continuity:

1. Foundation First:

- Begin with core customer information (names, contact details, account status)
- Establishes the new system's baseline functionality

2. Historical Integration:

- Migrate historical usage patterns and service records
- Ensures continuity of customer analytics and reporting

3. Real-Time Capabilities:

- Implement synchronization for current usage data and billing systems
- Enables live operations and dynamic customer interactions

Key Advantages:

- **Minimized risk** through gradual implementation
- **Continuous operations** with no service disruption
- **Progressive validation** at each implementation stage

This approach is particularly valuable for telecom operators requiring zero-downtime transitions while handling sensitive customer data and complex usage patterns.

Pros:

- Reduces the risk associated with large data migrations
- Allows for easier testing and validation of data integrity
- Can be less disruptive to business operations

Cons:

- Can be complex to manage, especially during the synchronization phase
- May require additional storage during the transition period
- Needs careful planning to ensure data consistency

Feature Toggling

Feature toggling is a technique that allows you to turn features on or off without deploying new code. In the context of legacy system modernization, it can be used to gradually introduce new functionality.

Here's how it works:

1. Implement the new feature in the modernized system.
2. Deploy the code with the feature turned off.
3. Use a feature toggle to enable the feature for a small group of users.
4. Gradually increase the number of users who have access to the new feature.

5. Once confident in the new feature, remove the toggle and make it available to all users.

Feature toggling proves particularly valuable when modernizing user-facing systems, enabling controlled rollouts and iterative improvements. A CRM dashboard update demonstrates this approach effectively:

Implementation Benefits:

- **Gradual feature exposure** (phased user group access)
- **Real-time feedback collection** from early adopters
- **Iterative refinement** before full release

Technical Advantages:

- Reduced risk through controlled exposure
- A/B testing capabilities for interface variations
- Zero-downtime deployments

This technique is especially powerful for customer relationship systems where user experience directly impacts productivity and adoption rates..

Pros:

- Allows for controlled rollout of new features
- Enables easy rollback if issues are discovered
- Can be used for A/B testing of new functionality

Cons:

- Requires careful management of feature flags
- Can increase complexity in the codebase
- Needs a robust system for managing and cleaning up old toggles

Best Practices for Legacy System Modernization

Now that we've covered the strategies and approaches for modernization, let's talk about some best practices that can help ensure the success of your project.

Start with a Clear Business Case

Before you embark on any modernization effort, make sure you have a clear understanding of why you're doing it. What business value will it deliver? How will it improve operations or customer experience? Having a strong business case will help you secure buy-in from stakeholders and keep the project focused on delivering real value.

Prioritize Based on Business Impact

Not all parts of your legacy system will need modernization at the same time. Prioritize based on which changes will have the biggest positive impact on your business. I always recommend creating a heat map that shows which areas of the system are causing the most pain or limiting business growth.

Involve Stakeholders Early and Often

Modernization projects can fail if they don't have buy-in from key stakeholders. Involve business users, IT staff, and executives from the beginning. Their input can be invaluable in shaping the modernization strategy and ensuring the new system meets everyone's needs.

Plan for Data Migration Early

Data migration is often one of the most challenging aspects of modernization. Start planning for it early in the process. Understand your data structures, clean up data where possible, and decide on a migration strategy well before you start the actual modernization work.

Maintain Business Continuity

Whatever modernization approach you choose, it's crucial to maintain business continuity throughout the process. Plan for how you'll keep operations running smoothly during the transition. This might involve running systems in parallel, planning for downtime during off-peak hours, or implementing temporary workarounds.

Invest in Training and Change Management

Don't underestimate the human side of modernization. New systems often mean new ways of working, which can be challenging for users. Invest in comprehensive training programs and change management efforts to ensure smooth adoption of the new system.

Implement Robust Testing Processes

Thorough testing is critical in any modernization project. Implement automated testing where possible, and plan for extensive user acceptance testing. Remember, you're not just testing new functionality, but also ensuring that all existing functionality works correctly in the new system.

Plan for Post-Modernization Support

Your work isn't done when the new system goes live. Plan for how you'll support the system post-modernization. This might involve training your IT staff on new technologies, setting up new support processes, or partnering with external vendors for ongoing maintenance.

Document Everything

Good documentation is crucial, especially when dealing with complex legacy systems. Make sure you document not just the new system, but also the modernization process itself. This can be invaluable if you need to troubleshoot issues later or if you undertake similar projects in the future.

Stay Flexible

Finally, remember that modernization projects rarely go exactly as planned. Stay flexible and be prepared to adjust your approach as you go. Regular check-ins and a willingness to pivot when necessary can make the difference between a successful modernization and a costly failure.

Conclusion

Legacy system modernization is a complex but necessary journey for many organizations. By carefully assessing your current systems, choosing the right modernization strategy, and implementing a phased migration approach, you can breathe new life into your aging systems and set your organization up for future success.

Remember, modernization is not a one-time event, but an ongoing process. The strategies and approaches we've discussed in this chapter should be part of your ongoing efforts to keep your systems up-to-date and aligned with your business needs.

As we wrap up this chapter, I hope you feel more confident about tackling your own legacy system modernization projects. It's a challenging task, but with careful planning and execution, it can transform your organization's capabilities and set you up for success in our rapidly evolving digital world.

In the next chapter, we'll look towards the future, exploring emerging trends in the software development life cycle. We'll discuss how developments in AI, machine learning, and low-code platforms are shaping the future of software development. So, keep reading to stay ahead of the curve!

Chapter 21: Future Trends in SDLC

As we conclude our journey through the Software Development Life Cycle (SDLC), it's time to look ahead and explore the exciting future that awaits us in the world of software development. In this chapter, we'll dive into the emerging trends that are reshaping the SDLC landscape, from the seamless integration of Agile and DevOps practices to the revolutionary impact of Artificial Intelligence and Machine Learning. We'll also explore the rise of low-code and no-code platforms that are democratizing software development. So, fasten your seatbelts as we embark on this thrilling ride into the future of SDLC!

Agile and DevOps Integration: A Match Made in Heaven

Remember when Agile was the new kid on the block, and everyone was skeptical about its ability to deliver? Well, look at us now! Agile methodologies have become the backbone of modern software development, and they're not going anywhere. But here's the kicker – Agile is getting a powerful ally in the form of DevOps.

You might be wondering, "Isn't DevOps already a part of our development process?" Well, yes and no. While many organizations have adopted DevOps practices, the future lies in the seamless integration of Agile and DevOps principles throughout the entire SDLC.

The Agile-DevOps Fusion

Imagine a world where your development team and operations team work in perfect harmony, like a well-oiled machine. That's the promise of Agile-DevOps fusion. Here's what this integration might look like:

1. **Continuous Everything**: We're talking about continuous integration, continuous delivery, and continuous deployment – all working together in a beautiful symphony. You'll be shipping features faster than ever before, with fewer bugs and happier customers.
2. **Automated Feedback Loops**: Picture this: You push a code change, and within minutes, you get feedback on its performance, security, and user experience. This rapid feedback cycle will allow you to iterate quickly and make data-driven decisions.
3. **Cross-functional Teams**: Say goodbye to siloed departments. In the future, your teams will be truly cross-functional, with developers, QA engineers, and operations specialists working side by side throughout the entire development process.
4. **Infrastructure as Code**: Remember the days of manually configuring servers? Those will be a distant memory. With infrastructure as code becoming the norm, you'll be able to version control and automate your entire infrastructure setup.

Combining Agile methodologies with DevOps practices can dramatically accelerate software delivery cycles. Organizations that successfully implement this approach often achieve:

- **Release frequency improvements** (from monthly to daily deployments)
- **Significant productivity gains** across development teams
- **Enhanced customer satisfaction** through continuous delivery of value

This fusion creates a competitive advantage by enabling rapid iteration while maintaining system stability and quality standards.

AI and Machine Learning: The Smart Revolution in Software Development

Artificial Intelligence (AI) and Machine Learning (ML) are no longer just buzzwords – they're becoming integral parts of the SDLC. As someone who's been in the trenches of software development for years, I can't help but get excited about the potential of these technologies to revolutionize our work.

AI-Powered Development Assistants

Imagine having a virtual assistant that can help you write better code, spot potential bugs, and even suggest optimizations. That's the power of AI-powered development assistants. These tools are getting smarter by the day, and they're set to become an indispensable part of every developer's toolkit.

Here are some ways AI will transform your development process:

1. **Intelligent Code Completion**: Gone are the days of simple autocomplete. Future IDEs will understand the context of your code and suggest entire blocks or functions that fit your use case.
2. **Automated Code Review**: AI will analyze your code in real-time, flagging potential issues and suggesting improvements before you even commit your changes.
3. **Bug Prediction**: Machine learning models will analyze your codebase and development patterns to predict where bugs are likely to occur, allowing you to proactively address potential issues.
4. **Natural Language Programming**: This one's a bit further out, but imagine being able to describe what you want your program to do in plain English, and having AI generate the code for you. It's not science fiction – it's the future of programming.

ML-Driven Testing and Quality Assurance

Testing and QA are areas where machine learning is already making significant inroads. In the future, we can expect ML to take on an even more prominent role:

1. **Intelligent Test Generation**: ML algorithms will analyze your code and automatically generate comprehensive test suites, ensuring better coverage with less manual effort.
2. **Predictive Analytics for Test Prioritization**: By analyzing historical data, ML models will help you prioritize which tests to run based on the likelihood of catching bugs, saving valuable time in your CI/CD pipeline.
3. **Anomaly Detection**: ML-powered monitoring tools will be able to detect unusual patterns in your application's behavior, alerting you to potential issues before they become critical problems.

Implementing machine learning in testing processes can deliver measurable improvements in software quality. Key benefits include:

- **Increased test coverage** (potential improvements of 30% or more)
- **Enhanced defect detection**, including critical bugs traditional methods may miss
- **More efficient testing cycles** through intelligent test case prioritization

This data-driven approach represents a significant evolution in quality assurance methodologies.

Low-Code and No-Code Platforms: Democratizing Software Development

As a developer, you might feel a bit threatened by the rise of low-code and no-code platforms. But trust me, these tools aren't here to replace us – they're here to augment our capabilities and open up new possibilities.

The Power of Visual Development

Low-code and no-code platforms are all about visual development. Instead of writing lines of code, you'll be working with drag-and-drop interfaces and pre-built components. This approach has several advantages:

1. **Rapid Prototyping**: You'll be able to quickly build and iterate on prototypes, getting feedback from stakeholders faster than ever before.

2. **Empowering Citizen Developers**: Business users with domain expertise but limited coding skills will be able to create simple applications, freeing up your time for more complex development tasks.

3. **Streamlined UI/UX Design**: These platforms often come with built-in design systems, making it easier to create consistent and user-friendly interfaces.

The Role of Professional Developers in a Low-Code World

Now, you might be thinking, "If anyone can build an app, what's left for us professional developers?" Plenty, as it turns out:

1. **Complex Logic and Integrations**: While low-code platforms are great for simple apps, complex business logic and integrations will still require your expertise.

2. **Platform Customization**: You'll be responsible for extending these platforms, creating custom components, and ensuring they meet your organization's specific needs.

3. **Performance Optimization**: As applications built on these platforms grow in complexity, your skills will be crucial in optimizing their performance and scalability.

4. **Governance and Best Practices**: You'll play a key role in establishing governance frameworks and best practices for using these platforms within your organization.

While low-code platforms enable business teams to rapidly develop basic applications, successful enterprise implementation requires addressing several critical factors:

1. **System Integration**
    - Seamless connection with existing infrastructure
    - API compatibility and data flow management
2. **Scalability Requirements**
    - Performance under expected user loads
    - Data storage and processing capacity
3. **Technical Oversight**
    - Architectural review of citizen-developed solutions
    - Compliance with security and data governance standards

This approach ensures low-code solutions deliver value while meeting enterprise technical requirements.

The Evolution of SDLC Methodologies

As we look to the future, it's clear that our traditional SDLC methodologies will continue to evolve. Here are some trends to watch out for:

Adaptive SDLC

The future of SDLC is all about adaptability. Instead of following a one-size-fits-all approach, organizations will adopt hybrid methodologies that combine elements of different approaches based on their specific needs.

For example, you might use a Kanban-style approach for ongoing maintenance tasks, Scrum for feature development, and a more traditional waterfall approach for critical infrastructure projects. The key is flexibility and choosing the right tool for the job.

Value Stream Management

Value Stream Management (VSM) is gaining traction as a way to optimize the entire software delivery process. VSM focuses on mapping, measuring, and improving the flow of value from idea to end-user.

In the future, you'll likely be using VSM tools that provide end-to-end visibility into your development process, helping you identify bottlenecks and optimize your workflow for maximum value delivery.

Continuous Everything

We've already touched on continuous integration and delivery, but the future is about "continuous everything." This includes:

1. **Continuous Planning**: Constantly refining and adjusting your project plans based on real-time feedback and changing priorities.
2. **Continuous Testing**: Automated tests running constantly, not just as part of your CI/CD pipeline, but throughout the development process.
3. **Continuous Monitoring**: Real-time monitoring of your applications in production, with automated alerts and self-healing capabilities.
4. **Continuous Learning**: Embracing a culture of continuous improvement and knowledge sharing within your development teams.

The Impact of Edge Computing on SDLC

As edge computing becomes more prevalent, it will have a significant impact on how we approach software development. Here's what you need to know:

Distributed Application Architecture

Edge computing will push us towards more distributed application architectures. Instead of monolithic applications running in centralized data centers, you'll be designing systems that can run partially on edge devices, closer to the end-user.

This shift will require new design patterns and architectural approaches. You'll need to think carefully about data synchronization, offline capabilities, and how to partition your application logic between the edge and the cloud.

New Testing Challenges

Testing distributed edge applications comes with its own set of challenges. You'll need to develop new testing strategies that can account for:

1. **Variable Network Conditions**: Your applications will need to perform well under a wide range of network conditions, from high-speed 5G to intermittent connectivity.
2. **Device Diversity**: Edge devices can range from powerful local servers to resource-constrained IoT devices. Your testing strategy will need to account for this diversity.
3. **Data Privacy and Security**: With data processing happening closer to the source, you'll need to ensure your testing covers all aspects of data privacy and security at the edge.

Edge-Aware CI/CD

Your CI/CD pipelines will need to evolve to support edge computing scenarios. This might include:

1. **Multi-Target Deployments**: Deploying different components of your application to various edge locations and the cloud simultaneously.
2. **Rollback Strategies**: Developing sophisticated rollback strategies that can handle partial failures in a distributed system.
3. **Canary Releases at the Edge**: Implementing canary release strategies that can work across a distributed edge network.

The Role of Blockchain in Future SDLC

Blockchain technology is set to play an increasingly important role in software development. Here's how it might impact your SDLC:

Smart Contracts for Automated Workflows

Smart contracts on blockchain platforms can automate many aspects of the SDLC:

1. **Automated Payments**: Smart contracts can automatically release payments to developers or vendors when certain milestones are met or deliverables are approved.
2. **License Management**: Blockchain can provide a tamper-proof record of software licenses, simplifying compliance and reducing piracy.
3. **Version Control**: While not replacing traditional version control systems, blockchain can provide an immutable audit trail of code changes and approvals.

Decentralized Applications (DApps)

As blockchain platforms mature, you'll likely find yourself working on more decentralized applications. This will require a shift in how you approach:

1. **Data Storage**: Instead of centralized databases, you'll be working with distributed ledgers and decentralized storage solutions.
2. **User Authentication**: Blockchain-based identity solutions will become more common, changing how you handle user authentication and authorization.
3. **Transaction Processing**: You'll need to design applications that can handle the unique characteristics of blockchain transactions, including latency and finality.

The Growing Importance of Cybersecurity in SDLC

As cyber threats continue to evolve, cybersecurity will become an even more critical aspect of the SDLC. Here's what you can expect:

Shift-Left Security

The "shift-left" movement in security will continue to gain momentum. This means:

1. **Security Requirements**: Security requirements will be defined and prioritized alongside functional requirements from the very beginning of the project.
2. **Threat Modeling**: You'll be conducting threat modeling exercises early in the design phase, identifying potential vulnerabilities before a single line of code is written.

3. **Security Testing**: Automated security testing will be integrated into your CI/CD pipeline, running alongside your functional tests.

AI-Powered Security Tools

AI and machine learning will play a crucial role in enhancing software security:

1. **Intelligent Vulnerability Detection**: AI-powered tools will analyze your code and infrastructure in real-time, identifying potential vulnerabilities with greater accuracy than traditional static analysis tools.
2. **Adaptive Authentication**: Machine learning models will power adaptive authentication systems, adjusting security measures based on user behavior and risk factors.
3. **Automated Incident Response**: AI will help automate incident response processes, reducing the time to detect and mitigate security breaches.

The Future of Team Collaboration in SDLC

As remote work becomes more prevalent and teams become more distributed, the tools and practices for team collaboration will continue to evolve:

Virtual and Augmented Reality Collaboration

VR and AR technologies will transform how development teams collaborate:

1. **Virtual Standup Meetings**: Imagine attending your daily standup in a virtual space, where you can interact with 3D representations of your project boards and metrics.
2. **Pair Programming in VR**: VR could enable a new form of pair programming, where developers can collaborate in a shared virtual environment, regardless of their physical location.
3. **AR-Enhanced Code Reviews**: Augmented reality could overlay code annotations and metrics directly onto your physical development environment, making code reviews more intuitive and immersive.

AI-Facilitated Team Dynamics

AI will play a role in improving team dynamics and productivity:

1. **Intelligent Task Assignment**: AI algorithms will analyze team members' skills, workload, and past performance to suggest optimal task assignments.

2. **Predictive Burnout Prevention**: ML models will monitor team metrics and individual behavior patterns to predict and prevent burnout before it occurs.

3. **Automated Meeting Summaries**: AI will generate comprehensive summaries of meetings, including action items and key decisions, ensuring that even team members who couldn't attend are kept in the loop.

The Impact of Quantum Computing on SDLC

While still in its early stages, quantum computing has the potential to revolutionize certain aspects of software development:

Quantum-Resistant Cryptography

As quantum computers become more powerful, they'll pose a threat to many current encryption methods. This means:

1. **New Encryption Algorithms**: You'll need to stay updated on quantum-resistant encryption algorithms and incorporate them into your applications.

2. **Crypto-Agility**: Designing systems with crypto-agility in mind, allowing for easy updates to cryptographic protocols as quantum computing advances.

Quantum-Inspired Algorithms

Even before true quantum computers become widely available, quantum-inspired algorithms are showing promise in solving certain types of problems:

1. **Optimization Problems**: Quantum-inspired algorithms could help solve complex optimization problems in areas like supply chain management or financial modeling.

2. **Machine Learning**: Quantum-inspired machine learning algorithms might offer performance improvements for certain types of ML tasks.

Ethical Considerations in Future SDLC

As software continues to play an increasingly central role in our lives, ethical considerations will become a more explicit part of the SDLC:

Ethical Design Frameworks

You'll likely see the adoption of formal ethical design frameworks as part of the SDLC:

1. **Ethics Checklists**: Just as you have security and accessibility checklists, you might have ethics checklists to ensure your software adheres to certain ethical standards.

2. **Ethical Impact Assessments**: Similar to privacy impact assessments, you might conduct ethical impact assessments for new features or products.

Algorithmic Fairness

As AI and ML become more prevalent in software systems, ensuring algorithmic fairness will be crucial:

1. **Bias Detection Tools**: You'll use specialized tools to detect and mitigate bias in your AI models and algorithms.
2. **Explainable AI**: There will be a growing emphasis on developing AI systems that can explain their decision-making processes, especially in high-stakes applications.

Conclusion: Embracing the Future of SDLC

As we've explored in this chapter, the future of SDLC is filled with exciting possibilities and challenges. From the seamless integration of Agile and DevOps to the transformative potential of AI and machine learning, from the democratization of software development through low-code platforms to the new frontiers opened up by edge computing and blockchain – the landscape of software development is evolving rapidly.

As a software professional, it's crucial to stay adaptable and keep learning. The skills that make you valuable today may not be the same ones that will be in demand five or ten years from now. But don't let that intimidate you – embrace it! The future of SDLC offers incredible opportunities for those who are willing to evolve with it.

Remember, at its core, software development will always be about solving problems and creating value for users. The tools and methodologies may change, but that fundamental purpose remains the same. So, as you navigate this exciting future, keep that user-centric focus, stay curious, and never stop learning.

The future of SDLC is bright, and you have the opportunity to shape it. So, go forth and build amazing things!

Book Conclusion

As we reach the end of our journey through "The Complete SDLC Handbook," I hope you've gained a comprehensive understanding of the software development life cycle. From the initial spark of an idea to the ongoing maintenance of a live system, we've explored every phase and nuance of this complex process. Remember, the SDLC isn't just a set of steps to follow; it's a philosophy that guides us in creating software that truly meets the needs of its users.

Book Conclusion

Throughout this book, we've seen how each phase of the SDLC builds upon the last, creating a robust framework for success. We started with the crucial task of gathering requirements, where I shared some of my own experiences in stakeholder interviews gone awry. From there, we delved into the intricacies of design, both high-level and low-level, where creativity meets practicality. The development phase brought us face-to-face with best practices and testing strategies that can make or break a project. I'm sure you can relate to those late nights debugging code, desperately searching for that elusive bug!

Deployment and maintenance might seem like the finish line, but as you've learned, they're really just the beginning of a software product's life. We've explored various deployment strategies, from the tried-and-true to cutting-edge techniques like blue-green deployments and canary releases. And let's not forget the often-overlooked but critical aspects of software maintenance and support. I still remember the first time I had to wake up at 3 AM to handle a production incident – it's an experience that truly drives home the importance of robust maintenance practices!

As we looked to the future of SDLC, we touched on emerging trends that are reshaping our industry. The integration of Agile and DevOps practices, the rise of AI and machine learning in software development, and the growing popularity of low-code and no-code platforms are all changing the way we approach software creation. But no matter how much the tools and techniques evolve, the core principles of the SDLC remain constant: understand the problem, design a solution, build it well, test it thoroughly, and support it diligently.

I hope this book has not only expanded your knowledge but also ignited your passion for software development. Whether you're a seasoned professional or just starting your journey in this field, there's always something new to learn and explore in the world of SDLC. As you apply these concepts in your own work, remember that every line of code you write, every design decision you make, and every bug you fix is contributing to something greater – software that can change lives and shape the future. So go forth with confidence, armed with the knowledge and insights from this handbook, and create amazing things. The world is waiting for your next great software solution!

www.ingramcontent.com/pod-product-compliance
Lightning Source LLC
LaVergne TN
LVHW080047210926
848481LV00011B/3297
* 9 7 9 8 2 3 1 3 2 3 8 9 0 *